RETURN OF THE ARTISAN

RETURN of the

ARTISAN

★

Grant McCracken

HOW AMERICA WENT *from* INDUSTRIAL *to* HANDMADE

Simon Element

New York   London   Toronto   Sydney   New Delhi

**SIMON
ELEMENT**

An Imprint of Simon & Schuster, Inc.
1230 Avenue of the Americas
New York, NY 10020

First Simon Element hardcover edition July 2022

SIMON ELEMENT and colophon are registered trademarks of Simon & Schuster, Inc.

For information about special discounts for bulk purchases, please contact Simon &
Schuster Special Sales at 1-866-506-1949 or business@simonandschuster.com.

The Simon & Schuster Speakers Bureau can bring authors to your live event. For more
information or to book an event, contact the Simon & Schuster Speakers Bureau at
1-866-248-3049 or visit our website at www.simonspeakers.com.

Interior design by Laura Levatino

Manufactured in the United States of America

10 9 8 7 6 5 4 3 2 1

Library of Congress Cataloging-in-Publication Data has been applied for.

ISBN 978-1-9821-4397-8
ISBN 978-1-9821-4398-5 (ebook)

To artisans, as they craft their past, present, and future

TABLE OF CONTENTS

INTRODUCTION

The return of the artisan is no small accomplishment. It is taking many thousands of people, starting up dairy farms, workshops, jewelry benches, bakeries, CSAs, chocolate factories, and Etsy accounts. It takes a quiet revolution in Berkeley, Boulder, and Brooklyn. It takes hundreds of thousands of people saying no to conventional career options and asking themselves if they might instead become a maker, an artisan.

And they are becoming increasingly visible. All those jams, cheeses, and handmade toys are beginning to nudge the conventional stuff off the shelves. An alternate world is opening up, and with it, a new idea is surfacing in our culture. Maybe manual labor is not the scorned, lesser work the twentieth century said it was. Maybe the dignity of running your own career, of shaping your own life, is worth the risk after all.

It's a shocking shift in thought. Over the past half century at least, we've become habituated to the idea of office work. For years it was the aspiration of almost everyone with a college degree. We became so very good at committee meetings, corporate-speak, annual reviews, feel-good picnics, and team-building exercises, it's a wonder we got any work done at all.

So a new model of work feels appropriately radical. The artisan doesn't wear a suit to work. She doesn't have an office or a parking space. She doesn't lie awake at night worrying about promotions. Her annual review is going to a local café with a friend and asking, "So how am I doing, do you figure? Be honest."

My answer: You are doing pretty darn magnificently.

We live in a time of large-scale, relentless change. We've all talked a lot about the technological driver of this change, the digital revolution that rewired the social world and gave us a new capitalism in the form of Amazon, Uber, and Warby Parker. Let's call this the digital disruption.

But there is a second, less-talked-about change. This is the artisanal disruption, the shift in what we want from our food, drink, family, community, economy. Thanks to the efforts of Alice Waters and other innovators, our world is moving steadily from the industrial to the handmade and human-scale.

The artisanal economy promises to change American capitalism. It is already giving us a new kind of consumer, a new kind of producer. But it's been a difficult birth.

The artisan discredits many things that took root in America after World War II: processed food, mass manufacturing, national brands, chemical and mechanical intervention, cross-country shipping, and especially the factory farm. (Many, in fact, believe that the words "factory" and "farm" should never appear in the same sentence.) After the hardships of World War II, we were thrilled to industrialize food. (Recall the popularity of Tang and TV dinners.) Now we are happiest when deindustrializing it.

The artisan does this one small enterprise at a time. They are taking up new kinds of work. They make cheese or soup or jam. They run a coffeehouse. They work as butchers or bakers. They run their own taxi service, thanks to Uber or Lyft. They operate a very small hotel, thanks to Airbnb. Remove the industrial layer of the American economy, and we find millions of small enterprises making their way in the world and in the process making a world for the rest of us.

INTRODUCTION

The Institute for the Future says:

The coming decade will see continuing economic transformation and the emergence of a new artisan economy. Many of the new artisans will be small and personal businesses—merchant-craftspeople producing one of a kind or limited runs of specialty goods for an increasingly large pool of customers seeking unique, customized, or niche products. These businesses will attract and retain craftspeople, artists, and engineers looking for the opportunity to build and create new products and markets.[1]

To be sure, capitalism will never lose its industrial foundations. We cannot hope to supply the world from cottage industries. Apple can take millions of orders for iPhones in a few days and deliver these phones in a month or two. This is an industrial system larger and more efficient than anything ever dreamed of by Adam Smith. But the industrial half of capitalism is losing its prestige and influence. Once great and grand, the industrial piece now threatens to become the "back office," the "infra-structure," the mere "offshore supplier" of capitalism. The public face of economics is increasingly a human, artisanal face.

The artisan experiment changes the way we think about daily life. And then it begins to change the way we think of our family, workplace, and community. It says that our locality should be more than the place we live. It says that capitalism exists to create not just economic value, but social value. The artisan says there are no "externalities," those brutal side effects of capitalism that we used to ignore. Everything that happens to us belongs to us. It's a single, seamless world.

There are two layers to the artisan experiment. In the first, we have all the exciting changes that innovators like Alice Waters brought to our local economies and our daily lives. In the second, we have the structural effects that follow from these changes, a transformation of the larger social and economic world.

As I say, we have a pretty good handle on the digital disruption, thanks to the work of folks like Clay Shirky, John Seely Brown, and Ethan Zuckerman. For the artisan, there is virtually nothing that gives us the big picture.[2] This book fills the gap. Without it, we are blind men and women in the presence of an extremely large—and growing—elephant.

But this book matters not only for intellectual reasons but also for practical ones. The small business is the great engine of our economy. It has created half of the jobs in the private sector and 65 percent of the net new jobs over the last seventeen years.[3] And at the heart of small business is the artisanal revolution. Increasingly, it is the font of value and the future of business.

But if the artisanal economy matters to small businesses, it matters even more to big businesses. The big beer brands, the big cola brands, and the fast-food companies, to name just three, are seeing their markets decline sometimes precipitously. And even when these companies try to adapt, they often get it wrong. The fast-food chain Wendy's introduced "natural fries," only to discover the nation was horrified by the "chemical stew" it took to prepare them.[4] The artisan says you can't just talk the talk. Cosmetic changes will not suffice. If a big business wants a place in our emerging economy, it is obliged to honor new principles. This means really understanding the movement.

And finally, the most urgent reason to understand the artisan option: we are watching the great tide of industry roll back, leaving millions of Americans without secure jobs or good incomes.[5] And when this happens, bad things follow. We have seen some small towns descend into social pathology, becoming centers of drug addiction and production, with citizens unemployed for years at a time.[6] The installation of artisanal economies and communities can help solve this problem by rebuilding both people and communities. And there is no value more valuable than this.

Some students of alternative movements scorn capitalism as the enemy, as the cause of every ill, as the very reason the artisanal movement is called for. They hope for the eclipse of capitalism, by a gift economy free of competition and inequity. I am not one of these people. What interests me about the artisan economy is precisely that it promises a reformation of capitalism, not the end of it.

I am sympathetic to those who long for a full-throated artisan revolution. That is the anthropologist's method: to grasp the artisanal disruption from the inside, from the head and heart of someone who lives there. But I wouldn't be doing my job were I not sensitive to the tensions and contradictions of the artisanal disruption. This book aims for a balanced view, sympathetic but not uncritical.

This book sees the artisan from two points of view. One of these we might call the Piper Cub perspective, the view from twelve thousand feet. We want to see the artisanal system as a whole, from farm to table, from economy to society, from the personal to the public. The other point of view sees things "up close and personal," as they play out in the lives of individuals. This is the artisan "on the ground."

I'm writing for two audiences: both the outsider and the insider. The insiders are those millions of people who have participated in some part of the artisanal disruption, from the artisan to the foodie to the crafter to the maker. This is a book for everyone who shops at a farmer's market or Whole Foods.

The outsiders are all those people who have heard about the movement and are curious to know more. There are two subgroups here: those for whom the artisanal disruption could serve as an employment opportunity in the postindustrial era, and boomers now poised for (and appalled by) retirement as their next "life stage." The artisanal disruption will give them both the big picture of this new economy, and the practical tips on how to become part of it.

The artisan experiment is not just about food and beer and spirits and cheese. It goes beyond the farmer's market and the coffeehouse. It's a social and cultural change that is transforming the whole American experiment. It's time we took a closer look at how this is happening and what we will look like when it's done.

1

THE BEGINNING

INDUSTRIAL AMERICA

Imagine this: We are piloting our brand-new 1955 Plymouth up the driveway of the Delamarre Hotel and Resort Complex in McArthur, New Jersey. Bellhops spring into action. Our bags are whisked away. With spouse and kids, we are here for a week, creatures of absolute, if temporary, privilege at one of America's best middle-rank resorts.

We can afford a week here because life is good. We were recently promoted to regional supervisor at our electronics firm, Hi-Fi-Stereo-Engineering. We have recently moved from an apartment in Canarsie, Brooklyn, to our brand-new suburban home in Hempstead, Long Island. The house, a ranch-style bungalow, is still waiting for the lawn and trees to fill in, but inside it's stuffed with new kitchen appliances, drapes, rugs, and furnishings, many made out of new plastics and miracle fabrics. In a place of pride is our fresh-off-the-assembly-line TV from RCA.

The memories of the war years are fresh, but we are working hard to forget the horror and privation. It helps that America is growing spectacularly. The mighty industrial engine built to supply the war effort is now turning out consumer goods of new quality and rising quantity. Science and technology are making good on the promise of progress. Disposable income rises steadily. Personal mobility is a structural fact of life. Intellectuals like John Kenneth Galbraith and Newton Minow are inclined to scorn our good fortune, but really, who cares? Modernist confidence, personal advancement, and the apparent triumph of the American economic model make this a happy time.

The Delamarre encourages our belief that 1950s America is the best of all possible worlds. It is outfitted with not one but three swimming pools, not one but two restaurants, both a full-size golf course and a miniature one, a "real" nightclub, and a racetrack for go-karts. If we like, we can pick up a courtesy phone and order a meal anywhere. An army of waiters stands at our beck and call. We can drink anytime we want. We can smoke anywhere we want. This is a place dedicated to our happiness.

There is one small worm in the apple. Well, it's a big worm, really. The Delamarre is a toxic place. It's so dangerous it might as well be sitting on an abandoned uranium mine. The ugly secret: the Delamarre is dedicated to the willing consumption of dangerous substances.

In the next six days, we will consume impressive quantities of sugar, fat, salt, sun, chlorine, nicotine, and alcohol. These are rough estimates.

Two adults over six days will consume:

> 240 cigarettes
> 6 bottles of wine
> 24 cocktails
> 12 after-dinner drinks
> 12 breakfasts
> 12 lunches
> 12 dinners
> 12 desserts
> 24 hours of sun exposure
> 6 hours of chlorine exposure
> 24 cans of soda
> 24 candy bars

By my inexpert calculation, this represents great whacks of sugar, fat, salt, alcohol, nicotine, and chlorine.

The family may have arrived at the Delamarre in a brand-new Plymouth, but some of them must have felt like leaving on a stretcher. This was a killing diet, not in the short term, but in the long.

A friend of mine recently found a box of film in her basement. One reel showed her parents at a cocktail party they had evidently staged in the backyard. Susan said that, at first, she thought she was looking at a gag reel. The men were all wearing flattop brush cuts and Hawaiian shirts. The women were wearing bright, sleeveless, A-line dresses. Martinis appeared to be flowing freely. What really struck her was that everyone seemed to be unbelievably good-humored. It was, she said, as if they were toasting something.

It's hard to know what Susan's parents were celebrating, but it might well have been their good fortune. After all, they had recently departed a cramped and noisy city life for bucolic suburbs. They were not alone. In the twenty years between 1950 and 1970, the population of the American suburbs nearly doubled, to 74 million. In the twenty years between 1940 and 1960, homeownership rose by nearly 65 percent.[1]

Some of this good humor may have come from the sheer joy of acquisition. The suburban home was new and it was filled with things people had never owned before: dishwashers, barbecues, stereos. And that was just for starters. Commercial art published by Fred McNabb in 1956 gave people an idea of what they had to look forward to: moving stairways, picture phones, even personal helicopters with a landing pad on the roof.[2]

A belief in progress was a core Western preoccupation for many centuries.[3] But in the 1950s this beautiful abstraction suddenly became a reality, driven by the accelerating confluence of commerce, science, technology, production, postwar optimism, and a newly vigorous marketing machine that produced glowing images like McNabb's own. People were primed for relentless improvement. The future drew closer with each new shiny appliance.

One of the things Susan's parents might have been celebrating was the electronic garage door opener, pictured here on the cover of *Science and Mechanics* in 1950.[4]

A garage door opener now seems a very commonplace technology. But for the reader of *Science and Mechanics* in 1950, it was a promissory note. An opener implied a garage, which implied a house, which implied a suburb, which demanded a car, perhaps one as futuristic as the one pictured on the following page. It was all so clear. To move out of the city brought you much closer to the future.

Thanks to the opener, the house bowed before your approach, opening like a drawbridge. Perhaps most thrillingly, the opener contained a push button, one of the celebrity objects of the moment.[5] Push buttons were progress made literal, bending the world to your will with the smallest physical effort. Just . . . push . . . a button and the world sprang into action, eager to do your bidding.

It is easy to think of all this simply as runaway materialism, and indeed, the intellectuals of the time exerted themselves to do just that. But the shiny objects were animated by large ideas.

By the mid-1950s, American cars were exhibiting the "forward look," thanks to the design work of Ned F. Nickles and Harley Earl, who pinched it from fighter jets they saw in World War II.[6,7] The eggheads saw this car as an exercise in conspicuous consumption and status seeking. But with the benefit of a half century of hindsight, we can now see that the forward look was designed to connect personal mobility to national progress, the advancement of technology, the promise of science, the drama of the Cold War, and the dynamism of the moment. Yes, these cars were inarguably status symbols; the new suburb was the perfect place

The garage door opener as celebrity tech in the 1950s.
Published July 21, 1950, copyright registration B249565,
Science and Mechanics Publishing Company.

to play out this ancient social motive. But their owners were also creating a new understanding of self, family, and society.[8] It matters here because it helped obscure the artisan impulse. This was our pre-artisanal "before." This is the world we eventually had to transcend to make way for the return of the artisan.

INDUSTRIAL FOOD

For the comedian Jerry Seinfeld, growing up on Long Island, there was something miraculous about Pop-Tarts.[9] He tells us that when he first grasped the reality of Pop-Tarts, the back of his head blew right off. What enthralled him must also have impressed the industrial engineer. Imagine the Pop-Tarts factory. You could load various raw materials at one end and out the other get a toaster-ready, shelf-stable foodstuff perfectly sized not only for the production line but also the package, the shelf, the shopping cart, and the grateful embrace of an eight-year-old. Pop-Tarts were the ultimate triumph of artifice. They were largely divorced from nature, virtually untouched by human contact, and mostly devoid of nutritional goodness. And they had the undying fealty of every American eight-year-old. For several decades after World War II, it looked as if no one, least of all the artisan, could challenge this hegemony.

Pop-Tarts made perfect sense to little Jerry Seinfeld. They came in two pieces because, well, a toaster had two slots. But of course, Jerry could not see the industrial agenda at work then. Pop-Tarts also took their shape and dimensions from the assembly line. You couldn't tell where it had been farmed, who had farmed it, or what, indeed, was in it. Somehow Pop-Tarts existed sui generis.

The natural environment of Pop-Tarts was not nature. It was the factory and the grocery stores. The latter was a veritable cathedral of light and color, with thousands of products laid out for viewing. All the brands were here: dinner in a box from Kraft, cereal from Kellogg's, soda pop from Coca-Cola, Chef Boyardee from American Home Foods, Cheetos from the Frito Company, all lovingly wrapped by design firms like Deskey and Walter Dorwin Teague, and promoted by advertising firms like McCann Erickson with inventive branding and relentless marketing.

To be sure, there was a small but persistent voice in the food community that scorned these products as mere delivery vehicles for salt, sugar, and fat. But the rest of America, recalling the deprivation of the '30s and the rationing of the war years, looked at them and said, "Oh, thank goodness."

Consumers wanted bright, shiny, immaculate, and clean. They wanted a world buoyed by optimism. They wanted a stream of innovation. They wanted to be pitched and wooed by Mad Men. Susan thought her parents might be celebrating something, and of course they were. Their world shone with beauty, novelty, advancement, indulgence, and solicitude. And at its height around 1963, this empire looked inviolable.

But quietly, the voice of skepticism grew. Leopold Kohr published his *The Breakdown of Nations* in 1957. Adelle Davis published *Let's Get Well* in 1965. Frances Moore Lappé published *Diet for a Small Planet* in 1971. Kohr's student E. F. Schumacher published *Small Is Beautiful* in 1973. Susan's parents may have heard these radical sentiments, but their response is not hard to imagine: "Small? Natural? For crying out loud, who wants to live small? Have you seen my RCA? Have you?"

There was an alternative to the supermarket. It was called the health food store. This was grubby, little, disorganized. Brands were badly designed, packaging was amateurish, quality control looked iffy, and a lot of things came in barrels. You just had to trust that someone was paying attention, and what if they weren't? Finally, it smelled. Consumers were bearded, sandaled, tie-died, and, yes, they smelled too.

It was a clear-cut David and Goliath story. In 1963, mass manufacturing, mass marketing, and mass media were so powerful they could literally tell Americans what they were going to have for dinner. This system made millions for executives and shareholders. Health food stores looked like an appallingly amateur exercise. Surely, this world was too little, too disorganized, too clueless, to take on and defeat the enemy.

Until it did. Toward the end of the twentieth century, it was increasingly clear who the winner was going to be. Grubby was going to triumph. The little world of natural, actual, unadulterated, unpreserved, untrucked food, this would win. Inexplicably, and against all odds, the food that threatened you with diabetes and early death was going to lose. People would fall out of love with the suburbs. They would begin to wonder whether the machine-made, the artificial, and the gifts of science and technology were really gifts at all. Everything that sang and shone in the 1950s now looked clueless, out of step, as dubious as the Delamarre Hotel and Resort Complex in McArthur, New Jersey.

The mystery: How did Americans pry themselves away from those beautiful supermarkets, that convenient food, those glowing packages, all that beloved sugar, fat, and salt? The answer: hippies persuaded them to adopt a different diet and a new way of seeing the world.

2

THE AWAKENING

HIPPIES AND THE COUNTERCULTURE

I n 1966, I was fifteen, living in Vancouver, B.C., and listening to a
drumbeat coming up the coast from San Francisco. My girlfriend had
a sister in her early twenties, and Nancy (not her real name) turned
out to be one of Vancouver's early hippies. Nancy let me stick around and
listen as her friends tested, and eventually mastered, the new ideas coming
out of California.

The budding anthropologist had a ringside seat! I got to hear people
argue why society was wrong in almost every particular. Fascinating! (I
had had no idea.) This was culture turning on culture. Hippies against the
middle class. Revolutionary zeal versus bourgeois stolidity. Wild acts of
imagination versus, well, bourgeois stolidity. Best of all, these ideas were
really going to antagonize my dad. Excellent.

Eventually, I got to see a second, tragic face of the revolution. Some
of these early hippies descended from drug use into drug abuse, and
then into heroin, and then into prostitution, and then, in some cases,
into suicide. If the early days of the cultural revolution had swept me
up, this dreadful end impressed me more. Perhaps human nature wasn't
malleable; perhaps the social order wasn't improvable; perhaps utopia

wasn't just around the corner, after all. This was a philosophical bucket of cold water for a kid just out into the world. What follows is tinged by this cynicism.

Hippies were shock troops in tie-dye, come to dismantle the consumer culture of the 1950s. They took aim at everything prized by Susan's parents. Those shirts and dresses? Ridiculous. The suburbs: tedious and conformist. The split-level homes: laughable. The cars: vulgar, showy, wasteful. The resorts: punishingly unspiritual, the perfect opposite of an ashram. The clothing . . . all those miracle fabrics, artificial colors, and life-of-their-own buoyancy. And what could be worse than "dry cleaning"? Coating yourself in polyester that was itself coated in tetrachloroethylene? What could be weirder?

For me, the best anthropological guide to the hippie revolution is a magnificent book by Donald Katz called *Home Fires*. This is a nuanced, unblinking treatment of the fate of the Gordon family. These days the counterculture is sometimes remembered as youthful high spirits and kooky good fun. But Katz shows the destructive fury the revolution unleashed on the Gordons. What began as a relatively happy, hopeful family living the good life on Long Island ends in disarray, damaged by a series of now-familiar misadventures. One of the Gordon children met with heroin addiction, tried prostitution, and contemplated suicide.

In some ways, the revolution portrayed here looks like a Western version of the Great Leap Forward being staged by Mao Zedong five thousand miles away. Children turning on parents. Youth cadre seeking to erase the traditional past from archives, temples, and homes. But of course, the Gordons were not the least bit Maoist. These Gordon children were not mesmerized by a totalitarian. They *volunteered* for the movement that destroyed their family.

Hippies were especially vociferous about food. It helped them make the case against American culture: The adulterants, the preservatives. The alienation of a natural substance from its natural state. The intervention of industry and marketing. The food of the 1950s was an obvious crime against nature. It was an indictment of capitalism (and whatever it was Susan's parents were doing in the backyard).

Had I been paying attention, I could report the hippie approach to food from my own experience. But I wasn't. What were the chances that I, as a middle church Canadian Protestant with Scottish, English, and American origins, would be anything but *insensible* when it came to the culinary? Happily, Jonathan Kauffman was paying attention and I have made his wonderful book *Hippie Food* my guide.

Kauffman looks at what food was like before hippies. He examines *The Good Housekeeping Cookbook* from 1963 and finds the majority of its recipes relying on food that came in boxes and cans. (Turkey Cashew Casserole called for canned meat and condensed cream-of-mushroom soup.) The "installed base" of '50s cuisine was formidable. To make reform harder still, hippie alternatives like tofu and tempeh were regarded with "suspicion and disgust." Organic farming was considered a "delusional act." Granola and yogurt were "foreign substances." This American food was well armored against hippie innovation.[1]

Eventually, hippie food prevailed. But Kauffman shows why this was not inevitable. Indeed, this food was, in some ways, so odd and unappetizing, it should probably have failed. Kauffman, bless him, does the anthropological thing: he asks people. The hippie food trend, it turns out, acted as both a provocation and a consequence of many other trends, including the Civil Rights Movement, the Vietnam War, and new ideas about ecology, women's liberation, black power, and personal exploration. It was especially instrumental in helping people make the transition from '60s politics to '70s culture. At one moment, it was driving the revolution; at another, it was a caboose in tow.

But of course, food was merely one piece of the counterculture. Crafts were also key. In the late '60s, a tidal wave of weaving, sewing, baking, canning, knitting, potting, planting, and carving was underway. Making things by hand at home, whether for your own or a neighbor's use, was virtuous work in a hippie community. Growing things counted too. Gardens flourished. Wall hangings, cork curtains, macramé baskets, tea cozies, found-in-an-alley art, plants, Indian textiles, Peruvian rugs, candles, and lots of cats—these were the signatures of the hippie household. All were auditioning for a place in the artisanal culture to come; only a few of them would make it. (Cats, sure. Cats go with everything.)

Hippies were hostile to technology. They regarded engineers as soulless bastards who wanted to subdue nature, equip for war, flatten city neighborhoods, create assembly lines, and otherwise enable the military-industrial complex. For hippies, technology was almost always the enemy. Rumor said a commune in the interior of British Columbia came up with a tech-free solution for stopping the truck after its brakes wore out. They ran it gently into a tree.

Of course, many hippies had overtly political aims: ending war and securing civil rights among them. But eventually, their aesthetic became more purely cultural. Todd Gitlin tells us that at a meeting in Berkeley in 1966 people stopped singing a union anthem, "Solidarity Forever," and started singing the Beatles' "Yellow Submarine." For Gitlin, this is evidence of a rapprochement of the political and the cultural, but it can also be seen as a premonition of the coming transition. Eventually, hippies would take their leave of the political, persuaded that they could do with culture what they could not do with politics.[2] As Stuart Brand overheard Ken Kesey say, it was important to observe the difference.[3]

The end of the hippie revolution was ugly. The price in suffering was high. If there is a single culprit, it was surely hard drugs. As Joe Samberg notes from his experience on San Francisco's Telegraph Avenue, the drugs designed to open the gates of consciousness eventually gave way to heroin. "All that stuff about consciousness was just sort of dropped."[4]

For other folks, the end was merely sad. Erika Anderson remembers her experience on The Farm in Tennessee as a "failed dream." For others, even the dream disappeared. These were kids who had read William Blake, listened to the Doors, and adored the Merry Pranksters, only to end up cleaning motel rooms in really dangerous parts of town.[5]

And sometimes, the end was simply weird. Take, for instance, the fate of Father Yod, who in 1969 founded The Source, one of the first vegetarian restaurants in Los Angeles.[6] One day in 1975, without training, experience, or explanation, Father Yod went hang gliding off a thirteen-hundred-foot cliff in Hawaii. He died nine hours later.

Still, the rudiments of the hippie contribution to the artisanal revolution are all pretty clear. The concern for transparency was fundamental. "Ingredients had to arrive in the kitchen looking like they were pulled out of the fields, not a package."[7] Removing intermediaries from the food world remains a core artisanal objective, as does getting rid of the branding and the marketing. Less is more. First, do no harm.

But there was one thing the artisan would not inherit from the hippie: the passion for aggressively altering consciousness. Caffeine is their god. Perhaps a little biohacking. An exquisite Gruyère? Soft drugs, maybe. Hard drugs, not at all.

On the whole, artisans also did not embrace the hippie hatred of capitalism. On the whole, they are okay with property, okay with capitalism, okay with technology. Artisans want to transform capitalism, to scale it down, make it less transactional and more social, less about economic wealth and more about communities flourishing. It is hard to imagine an artisan imitating Abbie Hoffman throwing dollar bills from the visitors' gallery of the New York Stock Exchange.[8]

Like hippies, artisans are not fans of hierarchical distinction. They don't cotton to elites. Neither artisans nor hippies aspire to empire building or social climbing. On the other hand, artisans are not quite as egalitarian as hippies were. They are especially prepared to acknowledge, and ever so subtly defer to, those who have taken their artisanal practice to uncommon heights. Master bakers and master brewers hold exalted status, and they carry themselves accordingly. They may treat us as equals in conversation, but everyone knows this is a gesture of kindness.

Artisans are more practical about politics than hippies were. They have no particular interest in communal undertakings. To be sure, there are some intentional communities that embrace a socialist logic. But most artisans prefer that old Yankee saying: every tub on its own bottom.[9] Individuals must stand on their own feet. Generosity is welcome. It's an effective way to build community. But it's optional, not obligatory.

In a sense, Kauffman's question remains unanswered. How did hippie ideas and ideals find their way from personal chaos, dissolute communities, and disagreeable foodstuffs into the mainstream? It's hard to say exactly. But they did. As a diffusion event, the long-term triumph of the hippie movement is astounding. It managed to go from thousands to millions of enthusiasts in not much more than a decade.[10] Even after the political movement fell away, its contribution to American culture lives on. When parents refuse soft drinks for their kids, when parents refuse fast foods for themselves, when schools refuse processed food for their students, that's the legacy of the hippie.

The end of the hippie movement was achieved in large part by punks and preps. Punks scorned the naïveté, the political cluelessness, the tender-hearted refusal to come to grips with the world. Preps scorned the sloppy sentiment, the refusal of social distinction, the woolly fashion sense, the hope that utopia could be achieved with music and drugs. Both disliked what they took to be the hippie's hollow piety.[11] But if the movement was dead, some of its ideas were locked into American culture, waiting there for the return of the Artisan.

3

THE PIONEERS

ALICE WATERS, STEWART BRAND, AND MARK FRAUENFELDER

Hippies hated technology for roughly the same reason Luddites did in the early nineteenth century: they believed it to be disempowering. To refuse technology was to show that you were free, while the rest of us were trapped in a vast exoskeleton of mechanical systems, technology, engineering, and artifice. It was a grand (and sincere) gesture, to be sure, but it left them at odds with the world.

And eventually, it left them tragically out of step with it. What began as a statement ended up a self-imposed curse: eventually you had no choice but to drive your truck into a tree. Before long, commune kids were returning from city visits all agog at how the cities hummed and bristled with machinery. (Elevators? Really?) Hippies renounced the world, only to discover that the world was quite happy to move on without them.

STEWART BRAND

Who would save them from their self-imposed exile? Stewart Brand would. Brand was the one who taught hippies to love technology—or at least to get out of the way.

First, he had the credentials. He was a hippie, at least for a time. Tom Wolfe found a shirtless Brand driving a Merry Prankster vehicle, wearing a shining piece of jewelry on his forehead and an Indian bead tie.[1] He wasn't a Prankster for long, Fred Turner tells us in his 2006 book, *From Counterculture to Cyberculture*.[2] Brand was like a comet. He entered worlds and then passed through them.

Before he was a hippie, Brand was a soldier (a parachutist, no less), and he believes that gave him a gift for organization that allowed him to help construct the counterculture taking shape in San Francisco in the late '60s. Brand organized the Trips Festival, a three-day event regarded by some as the movement's starter pistol.[3]

Brand was also a Stanford-trained biologist, which helped him understand big pictures and natural systems. He knew something about how events that begin in one part of the world could end up animating events elsewhere. (He was that animator.) As Turner deftly shows, Brand fashioned a connection between the counterculture and cyberculture.[4] (The rise of a cyberculture was inevitable. The form it took was not.)

Brand understood that NASA could take a photo of the entire Earth from space. And he could see what the photo might mean to a species that had spent most of its 6 million years on the planet captive of a vicious tribalism that made cooperation difficult, when not impossible. Brand felt certain that one glimpse of the Earth from outer space would change all this. "[N]o one would ever perceive things the same way."[5]

In January of 1966, Brand began selling buttons that read: "Why haven't we seen a photograph of the whole Earth yet?" He sold them at Sather Gate in Berkeley, wearing a top hat, white jumpsuit, and sandwich board. He was thrown off campus and spent the rest of the year selling the buttons everywhere he could.

Stewart Brand issues a challenge.

Brand was using the cheapest, tiniest form factor (a button?) to penetrate an air space filled with TV shows, ad campaigns, cereal boxes, billboards, coffee table magazines, and all that mass marketing on mass media. The nerve of the guy! Persuading a government bureaucracy to do something really hard and a little odd with a button that was badly edited, crudely made, and sold by hand in batches of one for a quarter. Yeah, right.

NASA finally took the photo in January of 1967. Brand used it as the cover for his next project, the *Whole Earth Catalog*. The *Catalog* was published several times between 1968 and 1972 and occasionally thereafter until 1998. It was a collection of practical things: diagrams, agricultural devices, tools, machines, seeds. In the words of *New Yorker* scribe Anna Wiener, it expressed "pioneer rhetoric, the celebration of individualism, the disdain for government and social institutions, the elision of power structures, the hubris of youth."[6] It was meant to encourage the reader in a liberal self-definition, a libertarian self-sufficiency, and a DIY presumption that the world wasn't really all that hard. (I mean, if you could use a button to get NASA to take a picture from outer space . . .)

This work was designed in part to soothe the hippie beast. As Walter Isaacson noted in his book *The Innovators*:

> The underlying premise was that a love of the earth and a love of technology could coexist, that hippies should make common cause with engineers, and that the future should be a festival where a.c. outlets would be provided.[7]

But if the *Whole Earth Catalog* looked back to hippies who were now in danger of losing touch with the wagon train of contemporary culture, it also looked forward to the personal computer revolutionaries who were well out ahead of it. (The *Catalog* wowed Steve Jobs and the founders of Airbnb, Stripe, and Facebook, to name a few.[8]) Brand was nothing if not fluid and multidimensional. He was various, not in that child-of-the-universe "look I'm a tree, now I'm a sunset" fashion of the moment, but as a creature of real multiplicity.

In fact, it's hard to find evidence of Brand ever repudiating anything. And this at a time when repudiating something was precisely the way you joined the counterculture and fashioned your identity. No, Brand kept everything—the Stanford training, the Army learning, the Merry Prankster bus rides, the rooftop visions—and kept going. In the late '60s and '70s, this meant he was visiting the emerging centers of computer research. His breadth of vision allowed him to see a possibility others missed: that what the communes were failing "to accomplish, the computers would complete."[9] That heady optimism is now hard to summon, but Brand in the 1960s could see it clearly before others could see at all.

The *Whole Earth Catalog*, that "way out" for hippies, became a "way in" for the computer geeks of Menlo Park. In the words of David Brooks, Brand "helped give tech a moral ethos, a group identity, a sense of itself as a transformational force for good."[10]

Today, Brand is occasionally criticized as a friend of capitalism and, gasp, individualism. (This is an odd charge to bring against someone who might as well be the poster child for individualism.) To quote more fully from the *New Yorker* piece:

> Certain elements of the "Whole Earth Catalog" haven't aged particularly well: the pioneer rhetoric, the celebration of individualism, the disdain for government and social institutions, the elision of power structures, the hubris of youth.[11]

Surely, this is ingratitude when directed against someone who gave us not just the *Whole Earth Catalog* but also the Trips Festivals, the *CoEvolution Quarterly*, the Hackers Conference, The WELL, Global Business Network, and the Long Now Foundation. Oh, and saved hippies. Ms. Wiener, please. (Talk about the hubris of youth.)

This is what Brand gives the artisan: a demonstration of what can happen once we step out of our endless cycle of self-reproach and forgetting. This is a deep piece of the evolutionary grammar of American culture. It's almost as if we can't move forward without scorning our past.

(This is indeed precisely what Wiener was doing for the *New Yorker*.) Too often, this leaves us forgetting what we know, willing a naïveté, and insisting on a clean slate when there remains a lot of wisdom on the existing one. Multiplicity is a Brandian gift and an artisan endowment. Why not use every bit of who you are, and what you know, in your work and art?

MARK FRAUENFELDER

Mark Frauenfelder can be seen as a lineal descendant of Stewart Brand. He's the editor-in-chief of a magazine (called *Make*), the co-owner of a blog (called *Boing Boing*), the founder of an event series (called Maker Faire), and he now works in an organization that resembles the Long Now (called the Institute for the Future). Publication in print, publication online, events, institutions cantilevered out into the future, and a feverish engagement with the world, it's all so very Brandian.

If Stewart Brand was proof of concept, Mark Frauenfelder is proof of practical possibility. And he is utterly and unapologetically post-hippie. The DIY ethos matters to him because it helps us "become more mindful of our daily activities, more appreciative of what we have, and more engaged with the systems and things that keep us alive and well."[12] Hippies wanted to see beneath surfaces in search of truth. Frauenfelder wanted to see beneath them in a search of a system. It's a difference that makes a difference. One looks away from the world, the other into it.

The Frauenfelder vision is anti-hippie in a second way. He describes a visit with friends Julian Darley and Celine Rich, founders of the Post Carbon Institute:

> They weren't blindly optimistic about going back to the land. Instead, they approached the problem as amateur scientists, using their

garden and workshop as a laboratory to test tools and technologies that might help people live in a world without cheap energy.[13]

Unlike hippies, the Mark Frauenfelder crew accept that the world has been shaped by the industrial revolution. Indeed, it is precisely this revolution that gives the DIY crew a puzzle to investigate and a method with which to work. The puzzle: the systems that keep us "alive and well." What are they? How can we use them? Could we do them ourselves? The method: mastering technologies and teaching the old dog new tricks. There is absolutely no "crash the truck" reflex here.

By the advent of DIY revolution, the industrial revolution was four or five centuries old. Machines were fully installed in the domestic world and our personal lives. They were now responsible for producing and preparing more and more of our diet. They were in our kitchens, garages, and living rooms. We were as gods, equipped with a push button.

Strangely, almost inexplicably, this marked a hiatus in our enthusiasm for the industrial regime. It was as if Baby Boomers said of tech, "Too close for comfort!" And when the hippie trickster bus drove past, they said, "Perfect. We can go back to the land. We can escape our technological nirvana. We can turn the clock back and pretend our industrial perfection never happened."

The gleam of that industrial perfection was already fading. At the very moment it was being celebrated by the people of the barbecue, their children were saying, "Absolutely not. We want to go back to nature. We want to go back to tribalism. Let's get out of here."

So Mark Frauenfelder and company had their work cut out for them. They wanted to revive the industrial after its hippie repudiation, even as they found a way to diminish, control, and reform it. They did this by splicing DNA from homo faber with that of homo ludens, in a laboratory accomplishment that would do much to shape the artisan.

Homo faber (forgive the sexist formula, please) is "man the maker." This creature knows the world by manipulating the world, by working with materials, seeking out combinations, creating mechanics in the production of outcomes. In the DIY version, this is a very manual way to know the world that wore its mechanisms on the outside, there for view, inspection, manipulation.

This homo faber learns by doing. This is often my experience of something new. It's only when I begin to use it that I begin to understand it. Or, better, I have to grasp it to grasp it. The DIY crew expect to see the mechanics of the thing and to work with those manually.

The DIY crew think of the world as a lab bench or the bricoleur's backyard. *What's here? What can I do with what's here? What can I make happen?* I remember reading about women who figured out a way to feed the dog in her apartment when she was going to be late getting home. The idea, and the tech, is now available to everyone at Maker Pro.[14]

One of earliest hacks was the Trojan room coffeepot created at the University of Cambridge in 1993.[15] This took a picture of the coffeepot and put it on the web, where it could be seen by Cambridge coders too lazy to walk to the end of the hall to have a look for themselves. The BBC gives us a more noble account: "[The Trojan room coffeepot] removed the need for any physical effort to check the coffee pot, and avoided the emotional distress of turning up to find it empty."

The Trojan room coffeepot charmed us because it was so completely pointless. Surely, it would be simpler to walk to the end of the hall and check, no? Plus, the coffeepot photo was so monstrously inefficient, insisting as it did on taking the long way around. A signal had to leap from a web camera onto the internet and find its way back again to computers just feet away. Who could keep from smiling at this combination of the breathtakingly possible and the completely unnecessary?

This is where homo faber begins to elide into homo ludens, "man the player." The bible here for anthropologists is Johan Huizinga's *Homo Ludens: A Study of the Play-Element in Culture*. Huizinga wanted us to see how much of human activity exists not for a practical purpose, but entirely for the heck of it. Released from necessity and practicality, most people (except, it turns out, Canadian bureaucrats) begin to make stuff up, easily and continuously and very, very happily. I was once in a brainstorm and sitting, it turned out, next to a banker. *Oh dear God*, I thought, *this is going to be a long day.* I was wrong. Within minutes she had entered Huizinga's state of play and was producing one brilliant idea after another.

Usually, there is a contest between these two creatures. Homo faber, on the one hand, tends to prize efficiency, precision, and rationality. She looks for the shortest distance between two points. She scorns things that do not cut to the chase and go straight to the problem.

Homo ludens, on the other hand, are interested in the imaginatively and intellectually possible. *Is this shimmering thought a good idea? Can it survive in the world without the oxygen supplied by the brainstorm?* Homo ludens don't care. It's enough that the idea exists, animating the world with possibilities, pushing people out of the proverbial box, releasing us from what the American anthropologist Clifford Geertz called the dead hand of competence and the recitation of the indubitable.[16]

They look mutually exclusive, but in fact, as Mark Frauenfelder shows, homo faber and homo ludens can coexist. In fact, there is no Trojan room coffeepot without the two of them working together.

The ultimate combination of the two came in the form of Rube Goldberg. Mr. Goldberg (1883–1970) was an engineer and a cartoonist.[17] He enjoyed enormous popularity in the first half of the twentieth century for the depiction of his fantastically complicated devices.[18]

By the 1950s, Goldberg and his cartoon creations were scorned as old-fashioned and just plain weird.[19] In a world of push buttons and brand-new kitchen appliances, Rube's technology looked gauche and pointless.

Then came the 1990s. Rube was back. His machines were everywhere—in dorm rooms, engineering competitions, music videos (OK GO), ads (Honda), and TV shows (*MythBusters* and *Elementary*).[20] Suddenly we were smitten by machines that threw unlikely parts into implausible combinations in a near-miss universe threatened constantly by pandemonium. We were in love with Rube again. Rube somehow "got us."

But, dude, like, why? We are well past hippie repudiation. We accept that tech must matter. Perhaps it's that we now suspect that tech matters too much. Thanks to the digital revolution, technology has gone from more or less dependable to almost always faultless. (FedEx delivers 6 million packages a day. When was the last time it lost one of yours?) We have only to think of something we need and, fourteen keystrokes later, it's on order at Amazon and, two days later, sitting on our doorstep. Digitally augmented, the machine is magnificent.[21]

That's why we love Rube Goldberg machines. They are so improbable in design, so tempting of failure. Our love of his machines reflects ingratitude born of anxiety. Something perfect in them is at odds with something in us. Years ago, I walked into a record store in Toronto. They were playing Bach on one of the first digital compact discs. "Listen to that," I said. "It's perfect." My friend paused and frowned. "Too perfect."

Right, I thought. *Too perfect. Poor us.*

Imperfection is now all the rage. That's why we love Rube's machines, tempting disorder at every handoff. And as the machines get ever more perfect, imperfection has become our difference, our signature. Or, well, it has to be. We will never again be as efficient as the machines. We might as well make imperfection our difference. It's how we do. We muddle through. We bumble on. C'est nous.

As the world is increasingly managed by digital perfection, the more

The Literary Digest for April 12, 1919

SOME CARTOONISTS WHO HELPED WIN THE WAR — CARICATURED BY THEMSELVES.

Rube Goldberg shows himself inking the air with a smoking pen.

we come to look like the odd ones out. Increasingly it looks like our world is actually the machine's world.

Imperfection is back in fashion. Even, God save us, for engineers. Jordan Vallejo of the Purdue Society of Professional Engineers was asked to identify her biggest challenge when making Rube Goldberg machines. She said:

> It's becoming harder to make these machines humorous and play-
> ful, but it's important to try. A lot of people think of engineering as
> a very serious career. Which it is! But it's important to take things
> lightly, to laugh, to learn from mistakes.[22]

That sound you hear is generations of engineers turning in their graves. Mistakes? Engineers don't make mistakes or, as Jack Nicholson says in *A Few Good Men*, people die. The idea that even engineers must show how lighthearted and playful they are tells us something about the world we live in now. Homo faber used to prevail. Now she must share the stage with creatures kooky and charming who help us learn from their mistakes.

So Mark Frauenfelder is riding a wave. DIY matters because it is an excellent way to embrace things that are defined by their imperfection, their near misses, their "OMG, I can't believe this thing actually works." But most of all, what matters about DIY tech is that we think with it, we tinker with it, we put it together, we do it ourselves. And this puts humans back in the driver's seat. Whew.

ALICE WATERS

Alice Waters opened her restaurant Chez Panisse in Berkeley in 1971. Inevitably, it became associated with the hippie moment. But it was also going to be an experiment within the experiment. Having studied

French culture at UC Berkeley and lived in France, Waters could see culinary possibilities beyond tofu, tempeh, and avocados.

The first order of business was to redefine food:

> [An] ideal was coming to fruition—French techniques pepped up with jazzy improvisation, bright-flavored and utterly fresh California ingredients, purity of flavor, simplicity of presentation, seasonality. This was the birth of what came to be called California cuisine.[23]

Beneath the cuisine were new principles: local ingredients, grown organically, harvested in season, taken straight to market, unadulterated by preservatives or industrial intervention. In a perfect world, the supply chain was a partnership, farmers working with chefs working with patrons, all committed not just to better dining but a new vision of food and society.

The restaurant was not an inevitable success. As Thomas McNamee puts it in his *Alice Waters and Chez Panisse,*

> How the slapdash, make-it-up-as-we-go-along little hangout and its harried mistress became such icons is a story of adventure, misadventure, unintended consequences, steel will, pure chance, and utterly unrealistic visions. The characters who thread through its history range from hedonists to Machiavellian careerists, from the crazy to the coolly rationalist; nearly all have been driven by passion, passion sometimes so fierce as to be blind. The road Chez Panisse has traveled from there to here is neither straight nor smooth. It is potholed, booby-trapped, cliff-hanging, devil-daring, sometimes not quite a road at all.[24]

The rise to greatness can be seen in the press coverage. The first plaudits appeared in the late 1970s. By the middle 1980s the *New York*

Times was prepared to celebrate Alice Waters for "revolutionizing American cooking." In 2001, *Gourmet* magazine declared Chez Panisse the "best restaurant in the US." Pretty good for a "slapdash, make-it-up-as-we-go-along little hangout."[25]

The hippie revolution was a groundswell. News traveled not so much by word of mouth as line of sight. Sometime in the middle '60s you could see new eddies forming everywhere in the fashion pond. Fabrics, colors, and styles of clothing were changing. Everyone seemed to be growing their hair long or at least "out." The hippie thing came up through the aquifer. Suddenly it was there.

Adopting the new look was easy. All we really needed to do was devolve, to repudiate fashion, propriety, status aspiration. The trick was to stop acting like the barbecue people and forsake those brush cuts and A-line dresses.

But the Chez Panisse revolution was different. It had to reach us by stages. It had to find its way out of Berkeley, a secret message traveling as if a sacred message, passing from one person to the next.

The Chez Panisse conversion called for knowledge and cultivation. It demanded that neophytes learn before attempting to teach. The restaurant might look like a funky old house on Shattuck Avenue embraced by a bunya pine. But it was also a seminary, sending waves of zealots into the world.

In fact, getting the message out of Berkeley was actually going to take an ecosystem of collaborators, what Paul Freeman calls a "network of chefs, activists, investors, and food enthusiasts."[26]

At the creative core of the network were Alice and her several collaborators and competitors, including: Danny Meyer, Ruth Reichl, Thomas Keller, Jeremiah Tower, James Beard, Mark Miller, Wolfgang Puck, David Bouley, Michael Pollan, Mark Bittman, and Jamie Oliver, among others.

There followed ten waves.

4

TEN WAVES
AND THREE TOWNS

A MOVEMENT GROWS,
FROM CONNECTICUT TO KENTUCKY

WAVE 1: THE CHEF DIASPORA

It was as if Waters were running a graduate school. Many chefs left Chez Panisse to start their own restaurants or auxiliary services. Mark Miller left to create the Fourth Street Grill, the Santa Fe Bar and Grill, and eventually Coyote Cafe. The year 1984 saw a sudden migration. Steve and Susan Sullivan left to open Acme bakery. Joyce Goldstein created Square One. Jeremiah Tower founded Stars. Dan Barber created the Blue Hill restaurant in Greenwich Village in 2000 and Blue Hill at Stone Barns in 2004. (My wife and I went for dinner at the latter. The room was crowded with waiters moving so expertly and effortlessly, I felt we had somehow ended up at the ballet.) The list is large: Suzanne Goin, Michael Tusk, April Bloomfield, Jonathan Waxman, Deborah Madison, and Dianne Dexter.

It would be wrong to think of these people as mere disciples, traveling like Thomas to spread the gospel in India. The Chez Panisse idea was still forming, still being crafted out of the experience of people on both sides of the house and, increasingly, across the country. Chez Panisse the restaurant would remain in Berkeley. Chez Panisse the idea would prove protein everywhere it ended up.

Chefs taught well and intimately. If you were a regular at a restaurant and if the house believed you grasped the experiment in play, you and your companion could hope for a visit from Chef. In the old days, this was a bit of flattery. An amuse-bouche to begin the meal, a small courtesy to end it. But the visit from a Chez Panisse graduate was more likely to include a discussion of the meal and the movement. This made the status compass spin in the other direction. In the old days a visit from Chef said, *Look, everyone, the chef knows me.* Nowadays it says, *Look, everyone, I know the chef.* Guests were touched by greatness, by knowledge, and, hopefully, not by Mario Batali.[1]

WAVE 2: SOME KEY COOKBOOKS

Cookbooks are a brilliant way for new ideas to find their way into the world. Here are some of the books that helped communicate the artisan message.

- Alice Waters et al. 1982. *Chez Panisse Menu Cookbook.* New York: Random House, 1982.
- Diane Rossen Worthington. 1983. *The Cuisine of California.* Los Angeles: Jeremy P. Tarcher.
- Jeremiah Tower. 1986. *New American Classics.* New York: Harper and Row.
- Norman Van Aken. 1988. *Norman Van Aken's Feast of of Sunlight: The Sumptuous Cuisine of Key West's Master Chef.* New York: Ballantine Books.
- Alice Waters and Paul Bertolli. 1988. *Chez Panisse Cooking.* New York: Random House.

- Mark Miller. 1989. *Coyote Cafe.* Berkeley, CA: Ten Speed Press.
- Ruth Reichl. 1998. *Tender at the Bone: Growing Up at the Table.* New York: Random House.
- Thomas Keller. 1998. *The French Laundry Cookbook.* New York: Artisan Books.
- Jeremiah Tower. 2002. *Jeremiah Tower Cooks.* New York: Stewart, Tabori & Chang.
- Michael Pollan. 2006. *The Omnivore's Dilemma: A Natural History of Four Meals.* New York: Penguin.
- Carlo Petrini. 2007. *Slow Food Nation.* With a foreword by Alice Waters. Translated by Clara Furlan and Jonathan Hunt. New York: Rizzoli Ex Libris.
- Alice Waters. 2010. *In the Green Kitchen: Techniques to Learn by Heart.* New York: Clarkson Potter.

WAVE 3: FIRST RESTAURANTS, THEN NEIGHBORHOODS, CITIES, AND ECOSYSTEMS

The first outposts of empire were the restaurants created by the outgoing chefs. Mark Miller's Coyote Cafe in Santa Fe was a seventeen-hour drive from Berkeley. Nashville and Pittsburgh, newly ordained as gastronomic destinations, were farther still.[2] In the early days, these were lonely places: tiny local radio stations, adored by their fans, but surrounded by Denny's restaurants, A&W outlets, and other acts of unforgiving skepticism.

Happily, like attracts like. If you bake it, they will come. Eventually, entire neighborhoods sprang up. Brooklyn was the first one that caught my attention. A friend observed that people there looked to him like survivors of the American Civil War and I thought what all anthropologists think in a situation like this: *A style of clothing might signal a style of life!* I went to look. Sure enough, Brooklyn was on a mission.

The experiment grew and grew. The Civil War metaphor got more and more apt. Brooklyn was a veritable munitions factory, lobbing brand after brand across the East River into Manhattan: Mast Brothers chocolate, Grady's Cold Brew, Brooklyn Brine Co., Kings County Jerky, Brooklyn Salsa Company. These started showing up on bodega shelves and then in bigger stores. They were little, earnest, experimental. Adoption would take a while. But the effect was remarkable. The inhabitants of Manhattan could hear something stirring.[3]

Innovation in Brooklyn was relentless. The old Pfizer pharmaceutical factory, closed in 2008, became a warren of artisanal innovation.[4] It had been purchased for this purpose by Acumen Capital Partners. For a building this size (a gigantic 660,000 square feet), it didn't cost much, a mere $26 million. But when capitalists invest, we know a movement is in motion. Brooklyn was becoming a parallel Manhattan, an answer to the question: What if New York City scaled down and scaled back?[5]

Eventually, entire towns were colonized by the movement. Boulder for instance. We only have to walk the streets there for a couple of hours to begin to feel like, *Yes, this is the way the world should feel.* We are surrounded by people who grasp the artisanal thing. And that's the moment the movement goes from ideal to idea to reality. *Right,* we say to ourselves, *it's a thing.* Soon after, *Right, it's the thing.* Eventually, we stop thinking about it altogether. We have a new assumption. It's only when we go home for Thanksgiving to a Butterball turkey, canned cranberry sauce, and green bean casserole, that we go, "Oh, right. America."[6]

Restaurants, neighborhoods, and cities together form an ecosystem. Take the case of the Loray Mill building in Gastonia, North Carolina. The mill was founded in 1902 and it grew to become, at six hundred thousand feet, the largest textile operation in the world. The mill lost its last tenant shortly after World War II. You can imagine the building as Joe Lenihan found it a decade ago: cavernous, decayed, and surrounded by a town in the clutches of a serious case of urban blight.

Lenihan rebuilt the place, filling that immense space with condos, a coworking space, an events space, a museum, a retail space, a place for farmer's markets, an incubator, an athletic club, and a place for artists and artisans. And with this, the town is beginning to come back. Perhaps the most compelling proof: Gastonia just built a new minor-league baseball field.[7]

WAVE 4: FOODIES

We have the diaspora of chefs. We have cookbooks. We have restaurants, neighborhoods, cities, and ecosystems. And, eventually, we have freestanding individuals to carry the flag. We call them foodies.[8]

Those conversations with Chef have an effect. The patron takes the gospel home. Buys a cookbook. Visits Brooklyn and maybe Boulder. Knowledge grows. Standards rise. The idea is now truly distributed, with thousands upon thousands of enthusiasts turned sometimes activists.

What are people talking about when they talk about food? Mostly, it's still a convivial conversation at table, over drinks, out with friends. But at some point, the foodie can be relied upon to tell the story of Alice Waters, Chez Panisse, and the artisanal movement. It's a diffusion cascade. One person becomes several people, and eventually everyone is working from the same hymnal. Conversation is the opportunity to not just recite the magic words but also engage in discussion that can actually reflect, and advance, the art and practice of this new thing coming out of California.

WAVE 5: MIXOLOGY

Sometime around the turn of the twenty-first century, after a grueling shift in the kitchen, chefs would go for a drink at their own or a neighboring bar. Inevitably, they would talk about the Chez Panisse mission. Bartenders are, by temperament and training, good listeners, and they found this chatter fascinating. The movement now leaps from food to spirits. Let's call it the mixology wave.

Bartenders were trapped in a stereotype, the one portrayed by Tom Cruise in *Cocktail* (1988), the flashy, bottle-spinning personality from whom a "Jack and Coke" was the best we could hope for. To be fair, they were working from a narrow menu and obliged to serve prefab combinations. Not much originality, nor even much thought, was called for. (Hence, I guess, the bottle spinning.)

As it happened, mixology was undergoing a transformation of its own. The key moment came nearly forty years ago when Dale DeGroff, working with Joe Baum, embarked upon a new approach to cocktails.[9] This was T+0 for the movement, the point of origin. Journalists in the person of Paul Harrington and Robert Hess signed on, and by 2001 mixology was on the map in Manhattan. Several bars sprang up, including Death & Co, Pegu Club, and Employees Only. An efflorescence took place in 2006, and places like Apotheke, Clover Club, and Drink emerged.

The mixologist was sometimes tormented by the new patron. In an article called "Has the Mixology Movement Created a Monster?" Camper English observed:

> Like the foodie movement before it, the recent mixology trend has created a new breed of patron, the kind who orders like this: "I'll

have an Aviation, the Hugo Ensslin version, but with Old Tom and Yvette instead of violette, so make it two-one-quarter-quarter. Luxardo, not Maraska, maraschino and who grows your lemons? If you have 2-inch cubes, I'll take it on the rocks, but not if you're using Kold-Draft. I know it's supposed to be served on the stem, but I'm sick of that Nick and Nora glass."[10]

Still, even this must have been better than the patron who treated you like a vending machine.

I remember the first mixology bar I visited. It was Drink in Boston, a place too hip to have a name on the door. I walked up to the bar; the bartender looked at me skeptically. (Nothing about my clothing says "hip" or "sophisticated." He was right to be suspicious.) I was about to order my usual, but he gave me a tiny shake of the head and a slightly censorious look. I stopped. (Canadians respond instantaneously to a censorious look.)

"How are you feeling today?" he asked.

"Um, fine?" I ventured.

He paused. "Happy, sad? What?"

I went with "happy." (I really wanted to go with "What?")

I came to understand that this was the new drill. My drink was to be handcrafted, according to my mood and the advice of my mixologist. No drink would ever be quite like this drink. I see that now. If this was a little precious, well, patrons were not the only ones making a show of their discernment. In some cases, the mixologist took pains to let us know how very lucky we were to have access to the depths of their learning. (I asked my Drink mixologist why my drink had square ice and he told me he preferred its "acoustical properties.") Sometimes the artisan is cheerful. Sometimes she is arrogant. This is a piece of the artisan experiment to which we will return.

WAVE 6: CRAFT BEER

The craft brewery movement wouldn't have flourished without an artisanal influence. These were two trends traveling in parallel. (And this is where we see the artisanal movement tapping something deeper than itself, the very bedrock of American culture.) They worked together, the Chez Panisse trend and craft beer did, two horses pulling the same troika across the wintry steppes of American hospitality.[11]

It turns out beer did small really, really well. Nanobreweries, microbreweries, craft breweries, brewpubs—if the artisanal is about being little and local, beer plays as well as or better than food. It turned out that there was lots of room beneath the reach of the mighty brands called Budweiser and Coors. An entire generation of consumers seemed to prefer brands that they'd only just heard of.[12]

Artisanal beer called for artisanal branding. Now designers aimed for names and labels that sounded vaguely nineteenth or early twentieth century. The recipe often involved something recently discovered in an old chest. The founders were working with inspiration from a distant ancestor often from the old country. Argh. The story got a little predictable.

The connoisseurship could be too, with guys (chiefly guys) rarely needing more than a couple of adjectives to salute the new beer. "Hoppy," "citrusy," were plenty. If you were really in a poetic mood, you could go with "biscuity." (This seemed to imitate the single malt revolution, where a lot of people got by with "smokey" and "peaty.")

If the Chez Panisse predecessor was an old-fashioned French restaurant with heavy red curtains and well-starched staff, the precursor to craft beer was a pub filled with career drinkers and college kids here to mix youthful spirits with their alcoholic ones. Craft beer gave rise to a more thoughtful producer, local celebrities, and places to drink that did not sneer at or obliterate more complicated conversation. It also produced a certain passion for the drink itself. What had once been simply a vehicle to supply alcohol to the bloodstream was now, increasingly, the point of the exercise.

WAVE 7: FAST CASUAL

Then came "fast casual," a trend the *Washington Post* called the "most important food trend" of the 1990s.[13] We could call this the artisanal trend coming to fast food—or better, what fast food was now obliged to do if it wanted to continue to prosper in American culture. Food was now made to order while you watched. Flavors were more complex. Branding and design more sophisticated. Ingredients were local when possible (which was actually not very often).

For some people, this was their introduction to the new kind of food. They knew strip malls. They knew fast food. But here were things like Chipotle (1993), Panera (1999), Shake Shack (2004), Eataly (2010) from Mario Batali, and Wolfgang Puck's Express at the airport. Each was a chance to try less-fast food. And while these places did not aspire to Chez Panisse standards, they did the invaluable work of inducting people into the CP conversation.

WAVE 8: WHOLE FOODS

Capitalism was beginning to see the economic opportunities in the artisanal. But there were several important barriers to entry.

Stores serving the artisanal market worked hard to reassure the shopper that they were not mainstream. This meant they refused the "big brand" approach to packaged processed food. For the millions of consumers who had been raised on vivid design and glossy packaging, these brands looked little, strange, and dubious, as if imported from Eastern Europe.

Whole Foods helped change this. Founded in 1980, it normalized health food. This meant eliminating the cultural baggage created by hippies. We could now change our eating habits without declaring a change in our life philosophy. Some consumers were not ever going to go to the artisanal. They would wait till it came to them. Whole Foods delivered.

The speed of Whole Foods' ascent is dizzying. It was started by John Mackey and Renee Lawson in Austin in 1978. It went public fourteen years later and was purchased by Amazon in 2017, when it was valued at $13.7 billion. It now operates over five hundred stores with sales of around $16 billion a year.[14]

The health food stores, once little, chaotic, and smelly, had been gentrified. Not everyone was happy about it. It is fashionable to say that John Mackey managed to destroy some essential part of the slow food movement. But then again, if artisans wanted to speak to a community larger that their local one, the John Mackeys of the world were essential.

WAVE 9: HITTING THE FOOD MAINSTREAM

Here's a moment from the anthropologist's notebook. You're doing an ethnographic interview in the home of a woman who is middle-class, middle-aged, and in most respects, to judge from the furnishings and art you can see around you, a person who belongs to mainstream America. All of a sudden, she calls herself a foodie.

You can't help thinking back to 1971, when Alice Waters opened Chez Panisse. Only a tiny handful of people grasped what she was up to. Fixed price, set menus, written in French by hand and changed daily, offering dishes that transformed Provençal cooking by letting in Californian light, beauty, and imagination. Most people had never tasted anything like this or indeed imagined it.

And then you think of all the things that had to happen, all the acts of communication that must take place, all the conversions that were called for, to get from the there in the early 1970s in Southern California to this here fifty years later in Columbus, Ohio. And if you stop being an anthropologist and start acting like an economist, you think of all the choices that had to be made, all the risks that had to be taken, all the careers ventured, the restaurants funded, the meals purchased, the reviews written, all the people who had to go, "Oh, that was good. More, please."

Every revolution begins with the conviction that the world will bow before its will. How often does it happen? Almost never. In American culture, there are maybe four other trends that have done as well as the artisanal food movement: hip-hop, the digital revolution in gaming, networking, and creativity, the new post-genre storytelling, the new expansionary selfhood, and that's it. Thousands of trends rushed into the world, aiming for the big time and the mainstream. Only five survived infancy to become redwoods in their own right. And one of these came from Chez Panisse.

How well did this trend do? In 2019, half of Americans called themselves foodies.[15] Whether they truly are foodies hardly matters. The movement is in full swing.

WAVE 10: AND THEN THE FLOOD?

All these waves ought to make a flood. But no. The old regime was powerful and well installed. Some American palates would scorn artisanal food. Some big-box stores would exclude it. There was still work to be done.

The organic market was making progress. The U.S. Department of Agriculture's (USDA) National Agricultural Statistics Service (NASS) reported 2019 sales of $9.93 billion in organic products, an increase of

31 percent from 2016. There were 16,585 certified organic farms, a 17 percent increase from 2016. There were 5.50 million certified acres, an increase of 9 percent over 2016.[16]

Perhaps the biggest indicator of progress was the purchase by big brands of smaller, artisanal ones. The fact that General Mills was prepared to buy Annie's Homegrown in 2014 for the princely sum of $820 million tells us that even big business now believed this market was robust.[17] CNN journalist Alicia Wallace said "organic products have gone mainstream" and they were now poised to penetrate the "neighborhood supermarket, the expansive discount store and the cavernous warehouse club."[18]

But there was bad with this good. In 2010, Frito-Lay started applying the term "artisanal" where it surely did not belong. Domino's launched a line of "artisan pizzas." This provoked death notices from Lewis Black and *Time* magazine. In 2013, *New York* magazine wrote wistfully of a pre-artisanal Brooklyn.[19] But we can take this abuse as a measure of the term's ubiquity. After all, Frito-Lay and Domino's would never use a term that was still obscure.

Handcrafted goods were also finding their way to a bigger market. Etsy was founded in 2005.[20] Forty-five million people made purchases there in 2019, and there were 2.5 million sellers on the platform. In August of 2020 there were 370,000 searches on Etsy for "personalized gifts."[21]

Ten waves are a lot of movement. But what does this tell us about the rise (and return) of the artisan? For some it's not enough merely to hear new lingo or see new restaurant preferences. They need evidence that the trend is reaching deeply into the way people live. Only thus can we say that the artisanal is more than a fad or fashion. Only then will the skeptic say, "I think we have something here."[22]

Let's look at three towns: Darien, Connecticut; Bowling Green, Kentucky; and Stamford, Connecticut. Our objective is to see whether and how the artisan trend works its way into the life of these communities.

TOWN 1: DARIEN, CONNECTICUT

Darien has 6,592 households.[23] It sits in the Connecticut panhandle forty miles northeast of New York City on the I-95 corridor that runs up to Boston. Houses are expensive; incomes are high; amenities are rich. There's a boat club, a yacht club, a hunt club, a social club, four country clubs, and eleven churches.

This is the Connecticut so hated by the avant-garde crowd in New York City and the pop-cultural one in Hollywood. On the one hand, they have portrayed Darien and neighboring towns as the home of robotic women (*Stepford Wives*, 1975 and 2004), anti-Semitism (*Gentleman's Agreement*, 1947), and desperate conformity (*The Man in the Gray Flannel Suit*, 1956; *The Ice Storm*, 1997; *Revolutionary Road*, 2008). On the other hand, the avant-garde and Hollywood never examine their own lives thus. When it comes to moral scrutiny, they tend to give themselves a pass. (Would the #metoo movement in Hollywood have been necessary otherwise?)

To see the old regime at its worst, we need to see what made Saturday night special. This Darien can be a place of unapologetic privilege, dinner with friends, at a table loaded with crystal, china, and silver. Hierarchical sensitivity, conspicuous consumption, insider self-congratulation, comme il faut conformity, an obsession with getting and spending, relentlessly anti-intellectual, anti-artistic conversation, and, above all, a smugness that does not know or care that, for the millions of Americans who endure poverty, the most extravagant meal on offer on Saturday night is a Big Mac.

This is the old Darien, the one now mostly past and largely scorned even by the locals. But not entirely. Darienites still gather some Saturday nights to scratch this ancient itch.

And that's where Ken Skovron comes in.

Ken runs Darien Cheese & Fine Foods.[24] He got started in the cheese business in the early '70s, when cheese making was an industrial enterprise measured more by the ton than the pound. "In those days," he says, "Jarlsberg was a gourmet cheese." He now works with small farms that make cheese by hand in a manner that's preindustrial. Jarlsberg is a distant memory.

The first thing that happens when you walk into Darien Cheese & Fine Foods is that Ken, his wife, Tori, or someone on his staff offers you a piece of cheese. Conversation ensues. Knowledge is imparted. After a couple of visits, visitors become a little more sophisticated. Many more visits and they stand ready to become connoisseurs.

Ken and company are good at scaling up this education by calibrated stages. And frankly, as an educational exercise it's not that hard. Virtually everyone in this community of lawyers, bankers, and investors is a good learner. They make distinctions for a living. Connoisseurship comes easily.

But Ken is not inviting people to enter the old temple of connoisseurship. Ken is dead set against the status competition that has ruled this town for so long. He doesn't want to impart knowledge that will be used as proof of social standing. When I interviewed him several years ago in the back of his always chilly store, he made this clear. His advice to his consumers: "Don't strive to be an expert. Be an enthusiast and keep on exploring. That's how you're going to learn. It's like a journey. Keep seeking, finding, and tasting." Connoisseurship knowledge is a way to show and garner status:

"Food was not meant to be treated this way," he [Ken] says. . . . "[P]eople [should] just land cheese on the table in the wrapper, open it up, and [say], 'Hey, we've got a great bottle of wine, we've got great food.'" It's not about serving the priciest Bordeaux. It's about "us talking, sharing a good glass of wine together, hanging out. We let our kids run around and play in the yard. . . [ellipsis in original] It's just about enjoying what it is, the beverage, the food, being together, people connecting again."[25]

Ken aims for the transformation of the dinner party. In the place of a table groaning with expensive things, Ken hopes that the event takes place around an island in a great room. Of course, stuffed with trophy appliances, the great room will be sumptuous in its own right. (This is Darien, after all.) But Ken sees the place as having a new tone. People are free to move about the kitchen.

Conversation is itself more mobile. In the place of smiling one-upmanship, Ken hopes people will talk about the cheese he recommended and move on to talk about . . . Well, who knows where it will end up? The status ritual is broken. Expensive things and exquisite choices matter less. If Ken succeeds, Saturday night will be less a theatrical production and more an exploration first of the palate and then of conversational possibility.

Under the relentless pressure of capitalism's "creative destruction," Darien's world is uncertain. Ken's customers have new and urgent things to talk about. Careers, enterprise, investment are all unstable, and up for grabs. In a sense, all Ken needs to do is to open a space. Once the status stuff has been cleared from the table, richer talk must surely flow.

Those who continue to fight the status battle are a little like generals fighting the last war. They are using the old armaments and strategies. They are still calling people uncouth, vulgar, arrivistes. But there is a new reality coming with a new set of damning keywords. Now, if you really want to diminish someone, you call them clueless or out of touch. Bankers, lawyers, investors can't afford "out of touch." Status may come and go, but in the knowledge economy, out of touch is forever.

Ken is, to this extent, a saboteur. Not a firebrand or revolutionary. But he is on a mission.

Everything about his work with cheese is unmistakably artisanal. No question there. No, the question is whether Ken is still being an artisan when embarked upon the reformation of Darien and the way this town socializes on a Saturday night.

Alice Waters, as nearly as I can tell, never talked about transforming social life or social elites. Her objective was to change the relationship between chef and farmer, farmer and land, farm and locality, and farmer, chef, and foodie to one another. This was how she aimed to be an agent of social change.[26]

Ken goes further. He is reaching into the social life of Darien to change in fundamental ways the way people think about what Erving Goffman called the "presentation of everyday life."[27] And he managed it. Darien is changing. Saturday night dinner is different. Conversation has evolved. All that noise created by status and its dictates ("I wonder if those linens are Frette"). All that is gone (or going). Now table talk is about the changing world of culture and the economy. Ken's vision of the artisanal transforms food, a community, and then some of the things it cares to care about.

If nothing else, Ken has helped make Darien a happier, healthier place. People take more pleasure in the moment. Their dining experience unleashes a mindfulness that lets them be a little closer to "being here now." And sharing really good food, he thinks, has the effect of making people more convivial. Actually, good food makes them good or at least better.

But is this proof enough for the skeptic? Are we really seeing a substantial change in a way of life and what we spend scarce resources on?

What truly has the artisanal revolution, as prosecuted by Ken and others, really meant to the deep character of Darien?

I think I have a compelling proof point. The good citizens of Darien are leaving.

My little town, Rowayton, sits just across the water from Darien. You could row across the Five Mile River in roughly ten minutes. Rowayton and Darien live cheek by jowl. It has not always been a happy relationship.

From the late 1880s to the early 1930s, Rowayton was a fairground town.[28] It featured the Roton Point Amusement Park, which had a roller coaster, a Ferris wheel, a merry-go-round, a dance floor, and visits from big bands like those of Glenn Miller and Duke Ellington. There were prizefights, beauty contests, and all the diversions that make a fairground a fairground: concession stands, a penny arcade, a shooting gallery, games of chance, junk food, and stuffed animals.

It was a noisy place. The town historian tells us that "[r]oller coaster riders screeched without restraint as the coaster dipped and plunged."[29] To make things noisier still, Rowayton was (unofficially) wet, when the rest of the country was dry. There are lots of little coves and bays that made it easy for Prohibition smugglers to spirit spirits onto shore. Rowayton somehow managed to look the other way when these and still less reputable economies sprang up.[30]

What did this all look like from the Darien side of the water?[31] Constant restless movement, crowds surging, things whirling and swirling. More to the point, what did it sound like? Well, you can imagine! A bloody great racket that seemed to go all night long, I can tell you!

Darien held its nose. Darien covered its ears. But there was no concealing the fact that Rowayton was a vulgar affront to everything decent people held dear and sophisticated people thought sophisticated. Rowayton would always be the distasteful, noisy cousin across the water. Even now, nearly one hundred years after Roton Point closed, feelings are still tender. Recently, a few good souls from Rowayton wondered if we should join Darien. The response from Darien was swift, snooty, and something like, "What makes you think we're a club that would ever dream of admitting the likes of you?"

Which makes it all the more interesting that, over the last ten years, some of the people living in Darien have been quite eager to move to Rowayton. They came seeking a redemption of some kind.

It's ever so odd. For starters, Rowayton is less well appointed. Darien has all those clubs. Rowayton has, let's see . . no clubs at all. No, that's not true. It has a beach club and a pocket yacht club noted for its "middle-brow ambience."[32] (That's Yankee code for "You would not believe the people they let into that place.")

Houses are smaller in Rowayton. The average size of a home in Darien is ten rooms. In Rowayton, it's five rooms.[33] Lots are smaller. Many Darien homes sit on an acre of land. Rowayton lots are so small a tractor lawn mower is sometimes not required. (I know!)

Why are people leaving Darien for Rowayton? A local realtor told me it's because of the "walk to town" trend.[34] I asked her why people in Darien didn't just walk to their own little town. The answers are telling. People don't walk very much in Darien. They are transported from their home to their clubs and back again. As if to discourage walking, there are very few sidewalks there. With big lots, it's a long way from house to town. And finally, by long-standing convention in this self-important community (and a large part of the rest of America, to be fair), walking was for losers.[35]

So what happened? What changed? People want to walk to town because they want to live where they reside. They want to make contact with local merchants. They want to chat with neighbors. As long as status was your raison d'être, you lived grandly to show your social standing and kept your distance. But now that social status matters less, the social world matters more. And this makes the grand homes of Darien an encumbrance instead of an augmentation. People matter more than things. Accidental contacts are preferred over the status tableaux of Saturday night.

Darienites are eager for smaller properties, smaller houses, and a smaller town because their places in Darien feel showy (even, a little show-off-y). Those vast lots felt isolating. It turns out Darienites were tired of merely waving to their neighbors. They actually wanted, sometimes, just sometimes, to talk to them. (I know, right?)[36]

We can't put this down to the Chez Panisse effect exclusively, or even mostly. It is a holdover from the counterculture. It owes something to the influence of Jane Jacobs and her well-publicized struggle with Robert Moses. It owes something to the mixed-use development trend that favors more urban, dense, and various. It may even have something to do with the bobo trend that David Brooks identified twenty years ago.[37] People want out of silos, into a neighborhood with a diversity of things and people.[38]

The question remains: Is "walk to town" the kind of evidence we're looking for? Does it say that people are hoping to live differently? I say yes. I think it says Darienites are looking for a life that is more social, intimate, and conversational. It changes us from creatures seen to creatures seeing.

But wait, there's more. People are not just leaving Darien to get out of Darien. They were also leaving Darien to get into Rowayton. Let me introduce you to a couple of people who come from there: Erin and Drew. They are architects of a different style of life, and they beckon.

ERIN

Erin moved to Rowayton from Brooklyn in 2008.[39] She took a fancy to the Rowayton Gardeners Club. With the help of Samira Schmitz and Tory Woodruff, she took control of the "Potting Shed" in the center of town and turned it into a kind of community center.

Erin decided to make an event for kids. In those days, local kids were on a short leash. They were the objects of helicopter parenting, and Erin figured that she could use the Potting Shed and its property to give them the chance to go a little wild.[40] Erin was right. The kids turned out to be eager agents of chaos and started turning cartwheels and brandishing sunflower stalks on the grounds of the Potting Shed.

Erin had a clear sense some parents were not happy:

Erin is accustomed to parents coming up to her and saying, "I'm so glad you do this"—in a tone that suggests they are anything but glad. The implication is, *This is really nuts and there's a good chance you are, too*. It's an ambivalence. These parents can see how much "sunflower combat" means to their kids, but they still find the whole thing a little bit, well, scary.[41]

This makes Erin a little like Ken. She wants to rescue kids from certain kinds of play, the way he wants to rescue their parents from certain kinds of hospitality. She has proposed a looser approach to child-rearing. Kids, she says, should play. She wants to make this town a place where the wild things are.

Does this make her an artisan? Well, not in a literal sense. It's not clear what she is making, unless we take a metaphoric leap and say "childhoods." But she is performing a social good that is entirely consistent with the Chez Panisse mission. Chez Panisse aimed beyond food to create social and cultural value, and, well, Erin is entirely keen on that. Without her, some local kids will be confined to playdates and helicopter parents, a house arrest that must serve them ill.[42]

DREW

Drew entertains a revolutionary impulse of her own. She has created a writing workshop called Taste Life Twice. She believes that ordinarily life rushes past us. When we write, she says, we relive. We get closer to the meaning of things. And that, she says, is a path to a truth.

What Drew doesn't want is storytelling that starts with something like "Jennifer was a woman in sorrow." We know where that's going. But if we choose a random image, say, "scraping Cheerios off a linoleum floor," that will take us any number of places, some of them sure to be illuminating. That's what makes Drew's class so useful as an opportunity for self-exploration.

Dinner parties can be predictable and confining. Certain kinds of childhood are also a kind of captivity, a block on creativity. And here too in the case of storytelling, we find a person, Drew, bent on an exercise that is designed to take us away from conventional into something more authentic.

Drew is aiming for mindfulness. Listening to her reminds me of the story about a conversation between two transcendentalists living in Concord, Massachusetts, in the nineteenth century. One says to the other that he's seen a young man sitting on a path examining a frog. The second man says, "Surely, that's not very odd." The first man replies, approvingly, "Yes, but he was still there when I walked past five hours later."[43]

To a transcendentalist, staring at a frog for several hours was an opportunity to remove the filters from sight and consciousness.

Americans are inclined to cultivate a swift self.[44] We believe that life is a smorgasbord of opportunities and that we must pursue them feverishly. This has the effect of destroying mindfulness and exposing us to burnout. We are moving so fast everything becomes a blur.

Drew's workshop is designed to make Americans more attentive to the moment. And this is surely one of the things the artisan hopes for. To encourage an attention to task that encourages a deep engagement with the material, the act, the craft, and the outcome. This is one of the things that distinguishes artisan craft from industrial production. Someone is paying attention, not just banging it out.

But is Drew an artisan? Yes, we could reach for metaphor again and say she is making stories and storytellers. She occupies the same space as

Ken and Erin, seeking to tear down certain conventions and set people free. Like Ken and Erin, she is creating an alternative to Darien dinners, childhoods, and stories. Everyone here is working on a new sense of community, authenticity, and self-knowledge. People are encouraged to take charge of the construction of the self. It's all so very DIY. In the case of Erin and Drew, there's no manual piece to the exercise, but everything else lines up with the artisan mission.

TOWN 2: BOWLING GREEN, KENTUCKY

Bowling Green is a town in western Kentucky of 68,500.[45] The largest employer here is Western Kentucky University, with four thousand jobs. The remaining industrial employers in the top ten supply a mere fifty-five hundred jobs between them. This is precisely the kind of labor market that provokes the rise of an artisanal economy. People invent their own work.

The tradition of individualism in Kentucky will surely help. You get a sense doing interviews. There's a small edge to the way Kentuckians tell you things. It's almost as if they're saying, "Go ahead, contradict me." There's no hostility, just fair warning. They are charming but steely. There's a subtext: *I am who I am. I am not obliged to care or accommodate who you are.* This "freestanding" quality is a good thing in an artisan.

But, I worried, what if I had merely been talking to a certain kind of person? Maybe my view of Kentuckians was not representative of the state. And then I saw a documentary called *Off the Grid.*

Thomas Massie is not from Bowling Green or even from western Kentucky. But he communicates the "freestanding" sentiment very well:

> My philosophy is live and let live and I think it comes from growing up here in eastern Kentucky where sort of the motto is "You don't

worry about what somebody's doing in their hollow, if they don't worry about what you are doing in your hollow."[46]

Massie went to MIT, invented new forms of virtual reality, and returned to live in Kentucky on a remote farm with his wife and two boys, entirely off the electrical grid. He captures his own water and solar. He raises his own food. Living off the grid put him at odds with a variety of regulatory agencies. They presumed to tell him how he should live. Massie took umbrage. Kentuckians applauded. Before you knew it, he was serving Kentucky as a congressman.

Massie gives off a simple, rugged individualism, but that doesn't mean he doesn't acknowledge a higher loyalty and a greater good. He is, after all, a Kentuckian. It would have been easy for a kid with degrees in both electrical and mechanical engineering, and a knowledge of virtual reality, to graduate and just keep going. Or he could have made Congress a springboard for his post-Kentucky future. But Massie always goes home to Kentucky. And what does he do there? He builds a self-sufficient farm on a distant hillside, well away from other Kentuckians. This is an artisanal tension: to be both freestanding and part of something larger.

Kentucky has other faces. Take, for instance, the Corner Store in Franklin. Strictly speaking, there is nothing artisanal about this enterprise. It is a classic corner store with all the usual things: newspapers, magazines, candy, coffee, Cokes, batteries, motor oil, mops, clamps, pliers, and cigarettes. There's cereal, Cheez-Its, instant coffee, and up near the ceiling a row of deer head trophies.[47]

Behind the counter, there's a giant of a man. (Only cliché can capture him.) Behind the giant is a sign that shows a handgun and the warning:

The average response time of a 911 call is 22 minutes. The response time of a .357 is 1400 feet per second.

Point taken. The giant supplies his own security. That's not artisanal either.

Where things do get artisanal is when the giant puts four tables along one side of the store. These are called liars' tables. "Why?" I ask. And I get a look for my trouble. Evidently, this is truth in packaging. People understand that men who gather to talk will end up lying. (Or at least "boast shamelessly, and make stuff up," especially when a good story demands it.) Everyone gets this. So let's just call it the liars' tables. (Canadians would never be this truthful.)

This makes this place a community center. Where would neighbors meet to talk in this county, if not here? This is a staging area. You go for smokes. Oh, there's your friend Jim. Sure, let's sit down and talk awhile. Someone joins you. Gossip pools. Speculation begins. Stories launch. Before you know it, everyone's lying their heads off.

You and Jim are sitting at a liars' table, so you have a license to let it rip rhetorically. It's even possible you have an obligation to go big or go home. Kentuckians and Canadian Maritimers have this in common: they are really good storytellers. They expect the listener to fall silent, and you almost always do because, quite clearly, a performance has begun, and before you know it you are completely absorbed.[48]

Storytelling is an artisanal activity. No, it doesn't make an object. But it does create something in the world, according to certain rules, to be judged by certain standards, that creates value out of its several effects. These are craftspeople. (Go ahead, tell them they aren't.) And they are good at what they do because they are constantly putting their work before other talented craftspeople, who either approve or don't.

Rhetorical criticism can be the kindest criticism. The listener who is unimpressed by the lie can simply withhold the usual nods and murmurs. The speaker doesn't have to take this to heart. She can merely suppose that the listener "wasn't really listening" or "never seems to get it any-

how." The Corner Store is a stage for artisans. If we were feeling pretentious, we would call their work spoken word. But of course, this is a more
ancient tradition, one that's been essential to the construction of self and
community here in Kentucky forever.

Erinn is a young woman telling stories with a purpose. She grew up
in eastern Kentucky, where, she says, she was touched by an "Appalachian
culture of despair." When she was in her early twenties, her husband fell
into opioid addiction. She became an alcoholic. There was no AA for her
in eastern Kentucky. But she did have a gift from her family. "My people
sit in a living room and talk." She decided to make this her path to sobri-
ety, her weapon against addiction.[49]

Erinn Williams, journalist and reformer.

Mountain people, Erinn says, are scorned as uneducated and un-worldly. "We don't venture outside the tribe." Erinn's plan was to give people a way out of this self-reproach. She does it with talk on and off the page.

She told me, "I'm different, and I know [my readers] can read me and feel that they can be different too. They can embrace the misfit within."[50]

Erinn writes for the *Times-Tribune*. Here's something she wrote in the summer of 2020:

I'm going to be vulnerable with you in this column, and open up to you about anxiety and fear. Neither of them are friends of mine. I felt the familiar wave of both edge nearer and closer as my chest has remained tight for several days. It's the worst feeling, truly it is. It comes and goes. Sometimes I'll go months at a time and not encounter it, I'll even forget it was ever an issue. However when it returns, it's horrible. . . . I consider you, the readers, to be friends, I'm grateful for the opportunity to share my feelings, thoughts, and fears with you. Even on days when my anxiety is through the roof, and fear is hovering like a fog, I find comfort in knowing my struggles are your struggles, and vice versa.[51]

Is Erinn an artisan? Her talk is authentic, transparent, open sourced, human scale, deeply personal, produces a cultural good, and solves a social problem. So, yes, Erinn is an artisan.

There are some activities that are closer to the conventional artisan model, and while they may have some pre–Chez Panisse precedent, they were surely accelerated by its influence. There is JD Country Milk, a small dairy in Logan County, Kentucky, that sells "real" milk, from pasture-grazed cows untouched by hormones, subject to low or no pasteurization, and sold in glass bottles at stores across the region. JD Country Milk is also the way that very small farmers find a path to market. Without JD Country Milk, certain local farms would perish.

The Home Cafe was opened in 2011 by Chelsey King and Josh Poling, both of whom trained at a culinary school and are determined to change Bowling Green cuisine with local ingredients in a local cuisine.[52] They were up against a formidable opponent: a local diet dominated by fast food and prepared food that leaves Kentucky with the eighth-highest rate of diabetes in the United States.[53]

Poling says cooking is, for him, a way of telling stories, especially his "love story" with Kentucky. He decided four years ago to start a new restaurant called Hickory & Oak:

> We tore down all these old buildings and now we realize we really lost a part of ourselves. I feel like when we stop serving a lot of the food we identify with, it's the same. I feel like Kentucky food shouldn't be known for chicken tenders. It has a beautiful food history and a beautiful food story. We're loaded with artisans. We're loaded with people who can naturally harness fire. From that fire you can smoke meat, you can grill meat. You can make sorghum. That's the idea of Hickory and Oak.[54]

Big American brands don't tell local stories. Artisans do.

There is a diverse group of artisans at work in Bowling Green now. Need More Acres is a farm run by Nathan and Michelle Howell.[55] They met at the University of Western Kentucky and decided that they would grow fruits and vegetables and, working with the meat, bread and dairy from other farms, create a Community Supported Agriculture program (CSA). They now serve thirty-five local families. Michelle says they do this to feed the "food desert" around them, to promote sustainability, and to be part of the farmer's market in town.[56]

*Nathan Howell at the Community Farmer's Market
in Bowling Green, KY (above). Brothers in Kombucha (below).*

There are two guys at the farmer's market who sell kombucha. They are still in school, still living with their parents. They see their product as a substitute for the carbonated soft drinks that put so much sugar into the Bowling Green diet. When I discovered that one of them had a business degree, I asked, "The difference between what you could make [at another job] and what you do make [selling kombucha]? That's a contribution to the community, isn't it?" Anthropologists are not supposed to lead the witness like this, but I wondered if these guys saw things this way. They don't.[57]

People in the artisan world in Bowling Green routinely make less than they could. We spoke to Kaelin Vernon, a farmer at Peacefield Farms who, with his wife, Heather, raises Leicester longwool sheep. These animals are so labor intensive the Vernons will never recover the time and money they spend on them. And apparently that's okay.[58]

It's okay because some larger good is being served. Kentuckians talk about this larger good in several ways. It might be God. It might be their Christianity. It might be Kentucky. It might be a shared pool of good fortune, the planet, the community, probably not in that order because, hey, this is Kentucky. (I did try to find out why Kentucky has such a powerful hold on the people who live there. The best answer: "Kentucky gives you a tattoo on the inside.")

My professor at the University of Chicago Marshall Sahlins would call this "generalized exchange." In a market economy, things are exchanged more directly, tit for tat. I give something to you only if I can expect something in return from you. That's "direct exchange." What interests Sahlins are the indirect exchanges, the ones in which we don't keep track of what we give and get. There's a feeling that it will all come out in the wash.[59]

Bill and Carol Greer, who run Top Crop Farms, are using generalized exchange. Volunteers help with cultivation of a garden plot. They give volunteer hours and they get the chance to work with the Greers' daughter Ginna, a special needs adult.[60] What the Greers gave was a vast investment of time to get Top Crops up and running. What they get, they hope, is a world where someone like Ginna will be more likely to be understood and accepted. But again, no one is keeping careful track.[61]

Derek Guyer runs Kentucky Reclaimed. It turns old tobacco barns into picture frames, Christmas angels, bookshelves, mantelpieces, and tabletops, selling to buyers around the country online.[62]

That's the business model. There's a moral model too, and that's all about "generalized exchange." What Guyer gives is emotional, social, and spiritual advice to the kids who work for him. He thinks too many kids get too little parenting. This son of a preacher likes to say he is "fishing for souls."

Saving souls with recycled wood.

And here's what Guyer says he gets. He owns this business in part due to the generosity of his workshop's previous owner. And what brought his business to life was a Wishing Well competition. Kentucky Reclaimed gives him a chance to involve his kids in a business. And it gives him a chance to reclaim a part of Kentucky that's otherwise "just gone forever."

From an economist's point of view, this is strange and wonderful. All this value pours back and forth between Kentuckians. It might as well be a great pool of oil sitting beneath the city. We don't have a way to measure and track this value. And people here couldn't care less. It's almost as if social good (as opposed to market good) is even better when we don't measure it. And it's okay that we don't get or give credit.

There is no local language for this exchange, no measures, no concepts. This is weird, because Americans measure everything, including pitch counts and thread counts. Surely, a measure for the good might be useful. But no, we just let this good flow into the world.

Bowling Green, Kentucky, takes its own path to the artisanal. People have set up coffee shops, food trucks, kombucha brands, CSAs. They are keeping bees, chickens, sheep, and cattle. They are making mead, soup, beer, nut bars, jams, pies, bread, bags, backpacks, quilts, furniture, wallets, belts, posters, prints, ceramics, stationery, furniture, and ceramics.

In the process, we have seen two things we didn't see in Darien.

Stories. People are telling stories, at liars' tables to build a local community, as newspaper columnists to heal the addicted, with food to fill the food desert, with wood to remember Kentucky's past.

Kentucky. People are pitching in for other artisans, saving or transforming Kentucky cuisine, saving or transforming Kentucky material culture, helping to raise sheep brought to the edge of extinction, making Kentucky a kinder place for people with special needs and a better place for boys who are under-parented. They are using it to get off the grid and to make a place for themselves well removed from other Kentuckians.

The artisan ethos fits in beautifully. Stories are artisanal. They help craft a world that is artisanal. The artisanal makes it possible for everyone to pitch in to help construct a Kentucky, that larger good that makes a pool from which people give and to which they give. (I don't think any-one in Connecticut ever does anything for "Connecticut." There are no internal tattoos there. Actually, not even on the outside.)

Big industries, tobacco and coal, have come and are now going. They left addiction and human misery in their wake. The artisanal option has sprung up to fill in. It serves in some of these ways in Darien, helping to craft a smaller, handmade, handcrafted, human-scale world. But here it is more something consumed than produced.

TOWN 3: STAMFORD, CONNECTICUT

I am standing in downtown Stamford, Connecticut, looking for Hi-Top Productions. I can't find it. I have been up and down Bank Street several times, which doesn't take very long, because it's only ten stores long.

What I can find is a barbershop, and what catches my attention is that this guy offers not just haircuts but shaves.

A little farther down is the Connecticut Cigar Company, and sitting in the window is a guy rolling cigars. Wait, what?

Stamford downtown is a grim place. It suffered the twin misfor-tunes of urban blight in the 1950s and later urban renewal designed to "fix" things. Which yielded the Stamford Town Center mall and a couple of other monstrosities. Together these forces managed to destroy almost every building of architectural interest, and all sense of place. Someone on Wikipedia thinks this makes Stamford look "more contemporary and modern" than other New England towns. Not really. Stamford looks like it has armored itself in concrete and prepared itself for war.

Stamford participated in the fury of innovation that made New

England the Silicon Valley of the nineteenth century. Industrial jobs were plentiful thanks to the production of dye, tools, stoves, typewriters, clothing, and the arrival of the Yale lock company.

But by the middle of the twentieth century, things began to conspire against the industrial base. Factory jobs went south. They went offshore. They vanished into the digital domain. Sitting against the highway that connects Stamford to New York in the west and Boston in the east, great towers demonstrate that this town still has great wealth. There's an enormous UBS building, a brand-new Royal Bank of Scotland, and even a glistening Trump condo to house those who don't want to commute from the city. But this prosperity belongs to someone else. Unless you are a participant in the knowledge, creative, or capital economies, Stamford is a tough place to find work.[63]

What doesn't exist here are a lot of factory jobs. Indeed, you could say that, in Stamford, people are coming back from the industrial era the way they once came back from war. They return to find the world substantially changed. There's no picking up where you left off, no getting back to "life as usual." If you want to work here, you're going to have to adjust and adapt.

For some, this will mean giving shaves or making cigars: a revival of the artisanal economy. Parts of Stamford are beginning to resemble the city as it was a couple of hundred years ago. It's a scaled-down world. What's missing is mass. And mass manufacturing. This is a world of small enterprise and "proprietors." People came back to find themselves in a pre-industrial Stamford. The industrial era is now for some but a dream.

Among the many things killed by the industrial revolution was the barbershop shave. This was still possible and popular as late as the middle of the twentieth century. (My evidence? That scene in *Chinatown*.) But after World War II, shaving in barbershops began to go DIY. Thanks to the safety razor and Gillette marketing, men came to assume that they should shave themselves. There was something uncomfortably intimate about one man shaving another. Plus, it was time-consuming and fussy. The modern gentleman (up-to-date and on-the-go!) preferred to shave himself.

And now the barbershop shave is back. Not everywhere. Not for everyone. But it's now possible to get a shave at Montana for Men on Bank Street, where "The Royal Shave" uses a steam towel and a straight razor. Will the barbershop shave ever reach the proportions of the nineteenth century? No. Should Gillette be worried? Not at all. But we can see this preindustrial operation as a sign of things to come. As people return from industrial service, they will, some of them, embrace an artisanal option.

And there is a lot to revive. Think of all those jobs in the nineteenth century that were artisanal in scale if not in practice. In the nineteenth century, people of a certain class and income didn't do much of anything for themselves. They didn't shave themselves. They didn't drive themselves. They didn't do their own errands. They didn't shine their own shoes. They didn't make their own meals. The clothes, food, and furniture didn't come prefabricated from great thundering factories but bespoke from now-vanished Victorian species: chauffeurs, butlers, tailors, dressmakers, maids, hatmakers, errand boys, bakers, butchers, tobacconists, shoe shiners, and barbers. Eventually, these jobs were swallowed up by DIY as supplied by mass manufacturers like Gillette.

Many of these jobs are on their way back. As more and more people "return" from the industrial era and contemplate their options, thousands will look for a way to evoke the artisanal option. There will be people rolling cigars, doing crafts, making pickles, soap, jam, and soft drinks, baking bread, brewing beer, crafting toys, driving food trucks. Some vanished Victorian species will come back to life.

THE POINT OF SALE

The artisanal economy continues to work its way through American culture. Having commandeered the restaurant and the bar, it takes on the local economy in Darien, Bowling Green, and Stamford. Consumers become producers, making artisanal makeup, candles, beauty products, clothing lines, pottery, and bicycles, and they sell these things via farmer's markets, craft fairs, Craigslist, and bulletin boards.[64]

The supermarket had come to dominate the grocery trade after World War II. By 1956, 90 percent of groceries were being purchased there.[65] In the early days, these places were welcome, even a little miraculous. They were endless yet somehow immaculate. Everything was beautifully designed and lit. (If you listened carefully, you could hear angels singing.) For some, supermarkets were the very image of American plenty. By turn of century, we were beginning to wonder if they weren't too large, too full, too illuminated, and too anonymous, and now a hymn to American artifice where once they had been a salute to plenty.

The farmer's market dramatically changes what people used to call point of sale. What is point of sale anyway? It's a figment of the mind of the marketer, that's what. Notice, it takes out everything, the people, product, context, tone, experience, social interaction, and social connection. Everything is out but the sale: national brands shoving for position, shouting for attention.[66]

The artisanal disruption has other ideas. It wants something that is bigger than a point and more complicated than a sale. The coffeehouse is no longer merely a place to transact the purchase of a caffeine-bearing liquid. In the right hands, it would become a community center, rich in poetry slams, art exhibits, and impromptu conversation of every kind on just about any topic. Farmer's markets are staged in some interesting part

Branding, the Farmer's Market way.

of town, the parking lot of the local library, say, or under a bridge down by the riverside. They offer turnips with dirt on them. They give us things sitting in rough baskets, on folding tables, with the people who did the growing, picking, or making standing there, prepared to say a word or two. There is no national advertising campaign, no big, bright visuals supplied by the ad agency, no blanching light of the grocery store. There's not even that convenience store smell that says, *Something died in here overnight. We just can't find it. Sorry.*

Now there's a person at point of sale. A human being being human, as the phrase has it. Not "spam in a can," in Tom Wolfe's famous phrase, not people who stand there, robotically hoping we will "have a nice day." At the farmer's market, people have personality, even if that means going on a little too long about a daughter's recent soccer triumph. ("Hey, check out her trophy!") That's a new price of doing business.[67]

Some neighborhoods moved so swiftly away from the supermarket they began to verge on a barter economy. You can see this in Portland, Brooklyn, Boulder, and, fleetingly, Burning Man. There is even an artisanal typeface for the sandwich board outside your shop. And they send these into exchange networks in the construction of a "shared" or a "gift" economy.[68] New collaborative resources pour in, thanks to Zipcars, Airbnb, seed swapping, crowdsourcing, community funding, and peer-to-peer cooperation of every kind. This artisanal capitalism lives cheek by jowl with industrial, managerial capitalism and is sometimes meant as a deliberate thumb in its eye.

Here, too, it's early days. But we expect these farmer's markets to supplant some of the dispassion, formality, and aridity we find at most retail. The "point of sale" is a high point of the artisanal economy.[69]

Just as important, or perhaps more important, the artisanal proposition seeks the creation of social value, where once economic value was enough. That café that roasts its own coffee beans started small and means to stay that way. Some of its work is to enrich the community. This is systematically different from boomer parents who went into business hoping Nestlé would buy them out. At the farmer's market, acts of production and exchange are, in Karl Polanyi's language, embedded in a larger world, and both constrained by and enriching of this world.[70] No reckless, red-of-tooth-and-claw capitalism here. Things get made. Value changes hands. But the exercise is incomplete until some social good is accomplished.

The artisanal economy threatens to divide the world in two. On one side, there's a village-like world, funded largely by sweat equity, imagination, and the wish to make the local community richer. On the other side, a forest of giant organizations like Unilever, Procter & Gamble, The Coca-Cola Company, and Nestlé, large and powerful, with market caps of $132 billion, $215 billion, $172 billion, and $267 billion respectively, working mostly for the shareholder. The artisanal economy seeks to remain small, personal, rooted in a community, and useful to people living there. Wall Street? At the extreme, an artisanal economy wants less to serve Wall Street than to occupy it.

The industrial half of this duality will never go away. We cannot hope to supply the needs of the whole world with tiny cottage industries. But the industrial half is in the process of losing its prestige and standing. Once great and grand, the industrial piece threatens to become the back office, the infrastructure, the offshore supplier to the artisanal face of capitalism. I think the corporate world can feel this transition taking place. And people on the inside are looking for ways to get out, to make their organizations more nuanced, more humane, and more human scaled.

5

THE RULES

TWENTY-FOUR THINGS
THAT DEFINE THE ARTISAN

1. IMPERFECTION

Artisans like the imperfect. We get a glimpse of why in a conversation between Mark Frauenfelder and his friends Eric Thomason and Julia Posey. Eric and Julia run an urban homesteading adventure called Ramshackle Solid, which experiments with gardening, crafting, beekeeping, and slow food, to name a few.

Eric said to Mark:

> There's an aspect of imperfection in the stuff we're doing—that's part
> of [our] name, Ramshackle Solid. I like imperfection. I like something
> that's been reworked or modified in an unintended direction and the
> way that that shapes the outcome of the project. . . . It seems more *real*.
> It seems more like it's a living thing or has a history at that point. If
> everything's perfect, it's kind of boring.[1]

For artisans, the imperfect has life. Perfection, on the other hand, is easy, and that makes it untrustworthy. Perfection is uniform, and that makes it a little tedious.

This concept also plays out in the world of the audiovisual. The objective of recording and reproduction used to be "high fidelity." Our standards rose steadily until we made it all the way to absolute fidelity. Then suddenly this wasn't enough. Now we were "Okay, then. That game is over. What can we learn from low fidelity?" Hence the return of vinyl.[2]

You may recall a moment in the 1990s when the Fisher-Price PXL PixelVision (aka the Kiddie Corder) became a celebrity object. A Canadian anthropologist was moved to remark:

> Now that we can capture a perfect image, the PixelVision seems to promise a larger, poetic truth. In a world of post mechanical perfection, we love the actual, the manual and the mechanical. It grounds us. It lets us back in. Most important, it flatters us. . . . Digital products are silent and slightly accusatory. They give nothing away about their internal operation, because frankly, they seem to say, you wouldn't understand it anyhow.[3]

Sara Winge was working in a technology firm in the Bay Area in the year 2000 when she noticed that a lot of her colleagues, people who made their living in the digital world, were now looking for recreation in almost anti-digital activities. These herders of perfectly orderly 1 and 0s were now keeping bees, raising chickens, working wood, smoking meats, and making kombucha. There was something rich and tasty about imperfection.

Imperfection is a theme in popular culture. We like the new TV because it is constantly breaking out of genre and doing messy things we can't anticipate. Trends in fashion and decor now favor the complex and unpredictable. Perfection is ordinary. Precedent is tedious. "Just so" is just so boring.

So artisans are in good and elegant company when it comes to imperfect. But I suspect they do not embrace it to be fashionable, but because they want to move toward what seems to them more real and authentic.

2. HUMAN SCALE

It's shiny. It's vast. It takes up many acres and contains thousands of people. It is the headquarters of the Procter & Gamble corporation in Cincinnati, Ohio. It seems to say, *Behold, we are magnificent. We are formidable.*[4]

There was a time when some people wanted all corporations to look like this. Size and scale were guarantors of seriousness, professionalism, and trustworthiness. We could depend on P&G. *Look at that building*, we said to ourselves. *They can't be doing this just for the fun of it.*

Compare P&G to Mary Lou Rankin, a ninety-two-year-old who makes fried apple pies in her kitchen and until 2019 sold them out of her son's store in Millersburg, Kentucky. Mary Lou started selling her pies forty-five years ago to benefit the local fire department. Until her retirement, she was selling around two hundred pies a week. Some people drive hundreds of miles to buy them.[5]

P&G headquarters and Mary Lou's home in Kentucky are the two extremes of the American economy. And not so long ago, P&G was the undisputed winner of the comparison. We wanted our corporation to be large and, yes, formidable. It meant we could trust them. It meant we should admire them.

By the P&G standard, Mary Lou was a hopeless amateur, a DIY embarrassment, a business so small it managed to be risible (when not invisible). I mean, really, making pies in your own kitchen? Selling them out of someone's storefront? Is this a business or amateur theater? Now we are charmed by the prospect of pie by Mary Lou. And, yes, some of us would happily drive a long way to get one.

Just landed.

The P&G building now looks like something out of *Independence Day*, the beginning of an alien occupation. And the metaphor gets more and more apt. These days it seems like P&G is so thoroughly out of touch with American culture it might as well be an alien occupation.

Somehow, the tables turned. The building that said, *You can trust us*, now seems to say, *We can barely conceal our contempt for you*. Human scale is a terrible thing to lose.

The artisan truth usually now sits somewhere in between Mary Lou and P&G. But it always prefers the former. The artisan enterprise will usually scale up to something bigger than a kitchen of a ninety-two-year-old woman. But this will always be its spiritual home: a single person working in a modest place, without the aid of any of the abbreviations that so adorn contemporary business: PR, HR, CEO, MBA, CIO, CMO, CCO. . . .

American capitalism has a tradition. People start companies with a view to scaling up and selling off. But many artisans establish an enterprise that aims to stay small. Here's the story of Paul Arney, the man who founded the Ale Apothecary:

> Disillusioned with his brewing job at Deschutes, Paul Arney quit his job there. With his wife, Staci, he then opened a brewery that would produce the antithesis of what he refers to as "factory beer." As much as their brewery outside Bend, Oregon, was meant to be an embrace of their ideals—freedom, craftsmanship, a sense of place—it was equally a rejection. It was built in purposeful opposition to the trappings of most modern American breweries. When the Ale Apothecary brewed its first beer in 2011, it had no stainless steel, no tasting room, and no staff besides Paul. He intended to keep it that way.[6]

As Paul found out, it's hard to stay small. Every artisan is running the ridge between not big enough to survive and too big to remain personal. What helps them find the balance is a sense of human scale.

For some people, it's a tension. Homa Dashtaki created White Moustache yogurt. She would like to scale . . . but she can't:

> For me, I just embrace that I have a cap. This is going to be a handmade product, and putting it in glass jars is super inefficient. Our label is super inefficient. I've just come to accept it, and now sort of take a sick sense of pride in it in a business sense.[7]

Capitalism prefers mass production, mass marketing, mass media, designed to speak to mass audiences. It wants to work at scale. Growth is regarded as manifestly good. By necessity and preference, the artisan often prefers a different approach. Happily, millions of consumers have also grown tired of mass and now routinely go shopping for small.[8]

As Steve King puts it, "small businesses define success idiosyncratically."[9] And that means there is no simple measure for the artisan, no easy way to say, *We're there. Stop growing!* Each artisan has to make their own decision on when this should happen, and it's a decision that will have to be returned to over and over. The irony is clear: The challenge of business used to be how to get big. Now, for some, it's how to stay small.

3. MAKING A HANDMADE PRODUCT

I have a piece of stone sitting on my desk. It's a Clovis end scraper. Many thousands of years ago, it was used to separate meat from hide.

It has a perfect weight to it. It's heavy enough to put some momentum into your swing, but not so heavy that cleaning a hide would wear you out.

I found it on a beach on the Long Island Sound. Just sitting there. Someone dropped it and it banged around in the sand and the surf for centuries. It could be very old. Scrapers emerged forty thousand years ago at the start of the Upper Paleolithic.[10] (I'm guessing this means the warranty has expired.)

To make this scraper, someone had to take a small rectangle of granite and give it seven new planes. Tricky. A work of very precise sculpture, without any of the tools now available to the sculptor. The maker was making something by hand that would help the scraper make two things by hand: dinner and clothing. Teaching the hand new tricks, that was the way we made a place for ourselves on the planet.

For a stretch of time so long it dwarfs our sense of scale, we made things by hand. It was only in the last several hundred years that we turned machines into an external self and asked them to take over. And, boy, did they take over. "Satanic mills" ran all day and night, turning the factory into a place with air you couldn't breathe and noise you couldn't stand. Increasingly, handmade goods were a reminder of "the world we have lost," as Peter Laslett called it, the world as it was before the machines came.[11]

The artisan works by hand. This is a guarantor of imperfection. This is true because most human hands can't make things without making them a little bit crooked. Hand work is charmingly crooked. It is also a guarantor of scale. Working by hand obliges us to keep it small.

Making things by hand is an almost eccentric thing to do when so much of our world is abstract and immaterial. Thomas Stewart introduced us to the idea of "intellectual capital." And we have been encouraged to think of our work as "digital content" created for an "attention economy" and a "creative class" in the formation of an "information society" and the age of the "Infovore."[12] All of this happens without hand work. (Well, except for the tapping of fingers on keyboards.) This work happens in the head, not the hand.

Handmade objects are material. They come from a hand. They come to rest in a hand. They act on the world through the hand. Much of the rest of the day we bathe in 1s and 0s streaming from computers, entertainment centers, and smart speakers. There is something more actual about the artisanal.

Matthew B. Crawford is worth reading on this and other artisanal matters. Here's what he says in *Shop Class as Soulcraft*:

> The satisfactions of manifesting oneself concretely in the world through manual competence have been known to make a man quiet and easy. They seem to relieve him of the need to offer chattering interpretations of himself to vindicate his worth.[13]

Crawford detects in hand work what psychologist Mihaly Csikszentmihalyi calls "flow."[14] This is the moment when we are so completely absorbed by what we are doing that we lose track of where we are in time and space. We can only stop the flow experience by falling out of the embrace of the moment. "Oh," we say. "Sorry. I was miles away." From a creative point of view, this is deep space, the place we are able to bring the best of our problem solving to bear on the problem at hand ("Should I cut it this way or that way?") and the larger issues of life ("How do I make myself make sense to a fifteen-year-old?").

As Crawford points out, we were inclined to scorn hand making in the later twentieth century. We got rid of shop class in favor of computer science and coding. We encouraged kids to give up trades for a berth on the global economy. Only lonely figures like Mike Rowe and his show *Dirty Jobs* were prepared to stand for manual labor. Otherwise, it was assumed to be beneath the dignity of anyone who aspired to the professional class.

Handmade things are material. But working by hand is an intensely cerebral exercise. We learn to make the hand sentient. Artisans "listen" with their hands. They "see" with their hands. For some, hands are the way to discover. We follow them to knowledge. They lead us to understanding.

There is a "conversation" between the hand and the material being worked. The craftsperson proposes a shape for the wood. The wood disagrees and makes a counter-offer. The two of them work out a compromise. This will sometimes rise to the level of inspiration. Neither party knew what would come of their interaction until, magically, something remarkable did.

But discovery and conversation don't stop when the artisan is finished. They carry over to the people who buy the object. They, too, now listen, see, and discover with it. They say the object is alive. They can hear it "speak." (Certainly, that Clovis scraper speaks to me. Mostly by saying, *Man, you have it so easy.*) We can hear the object chatter, murmur, declaim, according to the instructions of the artisan.

We admired how perfect things were when made by machines. Recall little Jerry Seinfeld's love of the perfect rectangularity of the Pop-Tart. Recall those toiletry kits that people used to bring home from trans-Atlantic flights for their kids. All sleekly designed with zippers and compartments and things inside. A dream for any eight-year-old, an immaculate creation, and now gloriously theirs, a promissory note from adulthood of the glamour to come.

But now we love things that are immaculate because they are untouched by machines. Once scorned, the manual is back. The handmade object can assume extraordinary powers. I wrote about these powers in an essay called "Uncle Meyer's Wallet," which is included in this book as the appendix. Decide for yourself.[15]

But even as we embrace it, we see the term "handmade" being called into question. Tito's Vodka is pitched as Tito's "handmade vodka."[16] Here someone sings the praises of salt that is hand panned: "The production of premium sea salt takes time and attention to detail. Each small batch of Balinese Sea Salt requires two weeks of hand panning and grading to produce."[17] Can the average person detect the difference when vodka or salt is handmade? There's no mystery here. Just marketing.

Anyone who wants a beautiful tour of the pleasures of the artisanal world should have a look at Handmade Nation. It comes both in a documentary (on Amazon Prime) and in the form of a book. It is absolutely chockablock full of illumination.[18]

4. CRAFTSMANSHIP

When the artisan crafts something in the world, inevitably she also crafts the personal self. She gives the self qualities. We have talked a lot about "externalities" in this book; let's call these qualities internalities.

When I think of an artisan, the picture that comes to mind is of someone working with her hands, head down, full concentration. This fashions the self wonderfully. It's a conversation not just between head and hand, but between some of who the person is, what she cares about aesthetically, and socially, and even commercially, and the object in her hand, the tradition in which she works, the way she is changing that tradition as she goes. There's a lot going on.

Often, the purpose of this process is to allow the artisan to resist mass culture. These objects are unique. They are made by someone as an expression of their uniqueness. And they enter the buyer's life as an exploration and augmentation of their uniqueness. Picture the moment of sale at the fair. A buyer swoops in and says, "I love this!" Connection made. Confirmation received. It also shows how the artisan resists mass manufacture. The triumph of the machine, the ability to make every object perfect and identical, for some part of the twentieth century this was a triumph. But by the twenty-first century we were wearying of it. Perfect. Schmerfect. Give us something with character, wit, and soul. The Renegade Craft Fair was established in Chicago in 2003 with the express purpose of encouraging a DIY aesthetic.[19] No to the machine made; yes to the handmade.

In the industrial era, when assembly lines were king, the producer wanted to be as machine-like as possible. The idea was to join the machine, embrace its discipline, efface our individuality, and create an object that looked like every object with this brand. In the post-industrial era, we embrace individuality and accident. Any given craft fair is a whirlwind of variety. There is no "quality control" in evidence here. The more individual, the better. The more ingenuity, the better. The more accident and variation, the better. Artisans harvest accident as if it were a blessing from the gods.

And for some, the artisanal process is a way to slow down their lives, to make a visceral, tactile relationship with materials and time. They are dispensing with the "hate my job, love my life" formula so common to office and factory work and instead aiming for something close to "love my job, love my life."

There is independence here of thought and action. I don't depend upon some larger organization, a creature that deigns to decide if I am worthy of employment, when and how I should be engaged, when and how I should be disposed of. In the words of Faythe Levine, craft is about "having control over my life . . . making my own destiny with what I create."[20]

Crafty lives are crafted lives.

5. RAWNESS

Years ago, I stumbled upon the opportunity to talk to chefs and find out how they were thinking about food. One of the people I talked to was Tyler Florence.[21] To be honest, I had never heard of him. But the moment I mentioned him to my wife, she looked at me with new regard. "Tyler Florence?" she asked, and then, just to make sure, "Tyler Florence?"

Tyler Florence it was indeed. We had a great conversation. He was generous and interesting. He talked a lot about his farm, the place from which he got most of the food he served at his San Francisco restaurant, Bar Florence.

"The important thing," he said, "is to get the farm right. I need to talk to my farmer. I need to make sure he's happy."

I wasn't sure what to ask next. I had always thought that a restaurant was really about the restaurateur. Or the chef. Not the suppliers. Not the farm. Not the farmer.

"And then my job is clear," Tyler continued.

I waited, hoping Mr. Florence would tell me what this meant.

"My job is to get out of the way."

This took me aback, captive as I was to an old-fashioned idea of the chef. I pictured someone large and, like, French, with a billowing white hat. I pictured someone who was kind of like an emperor—domineering, charismatic, and very grand. I pictured someone who did miraculous things with sauces and condiments. A guy who actually *liked* getting in the way, who actually believed that this was his job.

Clearly, this was not the Tyler Florence approach to things. For Florence, less is more. Adulteration is the enemy. Intervention, processing, preservatives, these are all bad. Raw is sometimes better than cooked. Sauces and condiments are disguises. A good chef lets the food speak.

Of course, the idea of unadulterated food can be taken to extremes. I had a friend in the 1970s who kept everything in the fridge in a brown paper bag. She did this because guru Adelle Davis had persuaded her that even exposure to light could damage the nutritional content of food. I didn't have the heart to tell her the light went off when the fridge door closed. But you could hear the philosophy at work. Untouched, unprocessed, unlit: "uns" were better.

In a way, "getting out of the way" might as well be a slogan for the entire artisanal movement.

6. LOCALISM

Artisans embed themselves in specific localities, which often puts them at odds with commerce, capitalism, profit, and growth. For an artisan, it matters where you are. It's the place from which you draw inspiration. Local communities are a big piece of why you do what you do.

But of course localities matter for another reason, as we learned from Alice Waters. It was Waters who declared war on the food industry and its love of vast quantities. This meant big factories. This meant central locations. This meant shelf stability. And it meant trucking things across the continent. All of which equaled the death of fresh.

Alice thought fresh was the way to make a meal. Don't go see what's in the fridge or the pantry. Don't go looking for a recipe. Go to a market and see what's fresh. Then eat that. Occam never had a razor like it! Eating fresh slays the dragons of industry in a single stroke, especially the trucking and the chemicals. Rarely had such a small idea made such a big change in the world.

Most of all, eating fresh gave the local guy a fighting chance. You had destroyed the advantages of big, centrality, and scale. The local guy could now compete. You would never get prices as low as what the industry could charge. But then, Alice suspected you didn't really want to eat what they were selling so cheaply. As she put it:

> If you wanted a peach that tasted like a peach, you pretty much had
> to grow it yourself.[22]

What happened to food also happened to beer.

Here, too, the magic year was 1971. As Alice Waters was establishing Chez Panisse in California, CAMRA (Campaign for Real Ale) was founded in Ireland by people who opposed the mass production of beer and the homogenization of the industry.

On the US side, 1971 was the year Frederick Louis "Fritz" Maytag III produced the first batches of bottled Anchor Steam from his newly reconstructed brewery, making it the first craft brewery since Prohibition to bottle its beer for sale.[23] Anchor Steam was an old American brand, founded in San Francisco in 1896, but it had struggled until Fritz's rescue. By the 1980s, the brand had become a national and industry influence, inspiring micro and craft imitators everywhere.

The growth in the American industry was remarkable. In 1979, there were 89 breweries in the United States. By 2013, there were 2,416. By 2019, there were 8,386.[24] It's among the purest instances of the triumph of the local.

Localism takes on another significance when artisans help build neighborhoods. Take the case of Olives & Grace, a tiny shop on Boston's south side. Sofi Madison created this store in order to bring artisans' goods to market. She moved here because rents were reasonable. The trouble is that Sofi's store and others like it have helped to gentrify the neighborhood, which has pushed rents up. And now Sofi may have to move on.

Sofi has a plan. With the help of other shop owners, she is trying to tell the artisanal story in a way that makes it clear to people who live in the neighborhood how much value comes from shops like hers, how these shops transform the local style and spirit of life there, and what happens when the big-box brands come in. (Reebok has just set up shop down the street, and while it is calling itself a collective, and trying its hardest, people are nervous.)

Sofi Madison is, in a sense, building the locality. Her store makes the neighborhood a better place to live. But, of course, she then has to sell the locality. She has to plead with people to understand why her things cost more. Effectively, she is asking people, *Where do you want to live?* Her argument, roughly, is you moved here because you found the neighborhood charming. But this charm doesn't happen by accident. If you want this place to remain charming, you know what to do. Patronize local shops. And not "patronize" in the diminishing sense, as in dropping by every month or so. No, make Olives & Grace the place you get your olives. Routinely.[25]

Artisans build localities. And these localities create many kinds of value, financial, emotional, social. It would be great if we could take a page from Sofi's world and find a way to talk about these at once. This is a job for a team of economists, anthropologists, and storytellers.

Marketing, the artisanal approach.

7. HAPPINESS

There's a guy in my community who's much happier than me. He is adored as a person, admired as an expert, respected as a teacher. He's a pillar of our community. He's an artisan.

His world is magnificently actual. At the moment, I am writing a sentence. No one will read it until agents, publishers, editors, designers, printers, bookstores, critics, and my wife have done their work. And that's going to take at least a year. Then the book will go out into the world and you will read it, if you read it, months or years later. Finally, unless you send me an email (and remember, you promised, the address is grant27@ gmail.com) I will never know you read the book.

Ken's world is a whole lot clearer. He gets to meet his "readers," (i.e., "eaters") as often as once a week. And they come in and say things like "I loved that Stilton you sold me. And that Arethusa cheese, wow!" Ken's satisfactions are a whole lot more tangible than mine.

Ken's world is also structurally straightforward. Thanks to the "creative destruction" of capitalism, as accelerated by a new order of innovation, competition, and disruption, many people in the bigger business world live a life of confusion and anxiety.[26] The possibility of having the world ripped out from under them is a distinct possibility. Most of the natural barriers to entry have fallen. And many managers spend their time wondering where the next hit is coming from. They know the target may not be their company but their job. Job security is gone.

Ken's world is clear. Yes, there can be problems in the supply chain. Yes, labor can prove hard to find or manage. But this is not an inscrutable world filled with big surprises or "black swans."[27] Compared to the sheer complexity of most middle managers, Ken's life is virtually contemplative. It is calm. It is composed. Most of all, it's transparent. Yes, it's true that some of Ken's clients make more money than he does. But it's also true that they pay enormous "transaction costs" to get this income and might well envy Ken. They might even someday even emulate him. (Some will join the artisanal disruption not out of necessity, but by choice.)

There's a last reason the artisan is happier than you or me. In the nineteenth century the relationship between Ken and me would have been a status relationship. The consumer was the superordinate. Ken was the subordinate. (Sorry for the sociological lingo.) The buyer ranked higher. The seller had to defer. That has changed beyond all recognition. Ken is a god in my community. I am but an ink-stained wretch. I make a point of letting people know that I know Ken. I would be very surprised if he ever tells anyone he knows me.

8. BEING FUNNIER (AND CHARMINGER)

Artisans are good at many things, but ingenuity is especially prized. Consider the case of the Postcard Machine (Possibly from the Future), which was invented by Michele Ott in 2006 and has since been installed at a variety of craft fairs and art shows.

The Postcard Machine is a "free-standing human-powered postcard vending machine." It is made from marine canvas and stands around six feet high, four feet wide, and three feet deep. (These measurements are guesswork.) The front of the machine shows a slot into which dollars can be fed. And it shows a slot through which, apparently, a postcard will eventually come. Even I could tell that this wasn't really a machine. After some reflection, it occurred to me that there must be someone inside the machine, taking money and giving cards.

The Postcard Machine is a parody of a vending machine. The vending machine came late in the industrial revolution. By the time of its appearance, machines had learned to do most everything: build, hoe, pick, dig, assemble, paint, finish, and distribute. What they couldn't quite manage to do was replace retail. They did not yet have a place in the general store, department store, or restaurant. They did not yet have a role to play at the moment of choice and purchase. And this made them very angry.

Then someone said, "Why not make a machine that can do what a Macy's salesperson does at the counter? Or what waitstaff do in a restaurant?"

And someone did. They invented the "Automat."[28] The first one in the United States was installed in Philadelphia in 1902. Patrons walked up to a wall of small compartments, inserted coins in a slot, lifted a window, and removed food. The machine was happy.

Did anyone ever protest this accomplishment? Did anyone ridicule the machine? Okay, sure, Charlie Chaplin in *Modern Times*, but who else? Michelle Ott, that's who. She de-mechanized the machine. Her machine was soft canvas and loving imprecision.

Having successfully ridiculed machine overreach, she took on what the corporation calls the value proposition. (This is the statement that captures what a corporation brings to the world, what they do for the world.)

Here's how Ott defines her consumer:

You love to receive tangible, wonderful surprises in the mail. You like to send notes to other people via the USPS. You write "thank you" cards to people. You put postcards on your refrigerator when you get them. You are kind to people. You are delighted to have a stack of blank postcards ready to write and send when the inspiration strikes. You love to support artists and are committed to helping them continue to make new work. You laugh at jokes. You appreciate astute observations of the world. You are my hero![28]

The conventional response to this sort of thing is to call it quirky. But that always seems to me a little patronizing and diminishing. Let's give Ott her due. Her postcards help us see things that capitalism can't see and, if left to its own devices, would render invisible.[29]

9. BEING HISTORICAL

I once met a Scottish stonemason wandering around a small town in Canada. He was staring at a local church. Closely, and for a long time.

"Hey," I said. An anthropologist is like a journalist: always on the lookout for a story.

"Hey," he said back in a rich Glaswegian brogue.

And that was all he had for me.

He kept looking at the church, his nose almost pressed up against it.

"Whatcha doin'?" I asked. This is the international call sign for *Whatcha doing?*

It worked.

"I'm having a look." He stepped back and stared up.

Then he said, "How old is this church, would you say?"

We scanned the front. No date.

"Nineteenth century?" I ventured.

"Obviously." He looked at me like I might be a little soft in the head.

Another long Scottish pause filled the space between us.

Then a burst of speech: "I think I can tell you that the masons who made this church were from Scotland."

"Really!" I exclaimed.

"Yes, really." You could hear an unspoken *chatterbox* here.

He continued, "I can tell you that they came from Scotland. I think I can tell you where they came from in Scotland. I think I can even tell you which part of Edinburgh they came from."

This is artisans talking to one another across 150 years and 3,000 miles.

An artisanal world stretches in two directions. One is the community of artisans in the present day. This is made up of all that sharing, comparing, competing, and learning. (Most of all learning.)

The other is the community over time, which stretches across centuries and continents. How long have humans been making beer? Probably 12,000 years.[30] When did we start making cheese? Artisans are time travelers. They can claim fellowship with communities and creativities that go back ages. By this standard, the blandishments of the mid-century modern, so sleek and abstract, so eager to claim the newest and the latest, all looks like slightly hysterical chatter.

For much of the twentieth century, we were particularly enamored of the new. In a wonderful book called *New*, Winifred Gallagher suggests we suffered "neophilia," novelty seeking and a craving for change.[31] This reached its peak sometime around 1960, when we were exhorted to throw off old things and buy new ones. There was actually something shameful about clothes that were "out of date." Out of date? This is not a concept that matters unduly in the artisan's world. But in the twentieth century, obsolescence seemed dangerous. We wanted to be "with it," whatever "it" was.

An artisan finds this weird. Historical is better, if only because it allows you to claim fellowship with all those artisans in Edinburgh who went before you. But also because history is a kind of ballast. It helps you steer a course. It helps identify what matters for moral purposes and what works for practical purposes. History is the artisan's laboratory. It's where she does her "time testing."

10. STAYING UNBRANDED

In the world of consumer-packaged goods (CPGs for short), brands were the way corporations let us know how good, nutritious, and downright miraculous their products were. Brands were beacons in the supermarket, shining from the shelf, charismatically colored, brilliantly boxed, irresistibly, er, irresistible! Now some brands are objects of suspicion, an act of trickery. We know too much about how the proverbial sausage is made; there is too little truth in its packaging.

Things in the farmer's market are trustworthier, because they are not branded. So much for Madison Avenue. All those millions of dollars poured into the brand as a marker of reliability, and we turn up our noses. We've come full circle; after all, in the eighteenth and nineteenth centuries, consumers were buying from barrels.

It turns out that Marx was right. (Finally.) The meaning of the object comes from the act of manufacture, not the act of marketing. It's as and when the artisan makes an object that she brings it to life.

Jocelyn Gayle Krodman doesn't have a brand. She doesn't need one:

> Jocelyn is an artist living and working in Kingston, NY. She created her brand, PetitFelts, in 2011 and since then she has made it her goal to create high quality, unique needle felted pieces. She strives to make animals that spring to life through their expressions and whimsical humor. She puts lots of love into her work and above all else, she hopes that people can sense that when they come across her creations.[32]

Jocelyn says she has a brand. But what she means is, she has a name. There's no real brand here, no logo, no packaging, no advertising, and no design thinking in a conventional marketing sense of the term. No attempt to mesmerize us with the Glenda the Fox brand. The idea of conventional branding of Glenda the Fox in a conventional way would seem as odd as branding a real fox. Everything that matters is the "love Jocelyn puts into her . . . creations." Glenda is the message and the medium. She doesn't need a brand.

A fox summoned out of felt.

Certainly, most artisan enterprises come with a story. In fact, this is getting a little tedious. It always seems to be about two guys who were sitting around one night and, what do you know, one guy says to the other . . . This is the origin myth of a cheese store (Beekman), razor blade (Harry's), bow tie (Two Guys Bow Ties), farm (Arethusa), and brewery (TwoGuys Brewing). Not that this is a bad thing. Everyone needs a story. But wouldn't it be good if it weren't always the same story?

11. STORIES

What artisans have instead of brands are stories. And yes, these can be clichéd, as in the case of the "two guys who had an idea." Every artisan surely has more to draw on than the origin myth. What about all that trial and error? Triumph and heartbreak? Being agile, nimble, adaptive, and responsive? All those buzzwords from the corporate handbook, so much talked about and often so little practiced, are alive and well in the world of the artisan. Let's tell those stories more.

Plus, there is almost no artisanal knowledge that does not come wrapped in a story. I don't remember "the way to shear a Leicester long-wool sheep." I remember the guy, Kaelin Vernon, who told me how he does that, the farm he and his wife live on in Plano County, even per-haps the weather on the day I talked to him (wet and muddy). Artisanal knowledge is personal knowledge.

Artisanal knowledge is embedded knowledge. That tool on some-one's workbench comes from a great-grandfather and memorializes how he started a family tradition. The bridge that stands in the center of town evokes how this community pitches in and works together. No plaque. No opening ceremony. No yearly ritual. You see the bridge, you think of the meetings and the work and how much better life got when the bridge went in.

Stories also prove to be an alternative to brand marketing. Where the typical consumer product will build a brand and beat the marketing drum, the artisan must resort to other options. Happily, these aren't just cheaper; they are distinctly better.

Take the case of Lacey, the Media Wonder Dog. Lacey lives on the farm of James Beckner and Robin Harden. This is James's family farm, and it is a miracle of initiative. Rock'n B Farm offers carriage rides,

Christmas gatherings, "fire-pit to pan" dinners, Fall Festivals, Valentine's Day celebrations, outdoor weddings, and any other social event that looks like it might draw an audience. James and Robin, ever resourceful and ingenious, also built Mammaws Kitchen on the back of their farmhouse. I dropped in for lunch a couple of years ago and we were greeted almost immediately by Lacey.

Lacey looks like a standard sheepdog, but she is in fact a marketing genius, a story that cannot wait to be told. James is occasionally asked to do a spot on local TV. He takes Lacey along because, well, Lacey is the star. Everyone at the studio drops by to welcome her. She gets her own chair on camera and most of the close-ups. When people come to the farm, they all want to see Lacey. As a gifted sales creature, she likes to jump up and establish full eye contact.[33]

There are many alternatives to conventional marketing. Lacey is merely a very cute one. The trick is to turn the stories that define that artisan's life and communities into stories the rest of the world wants to share.

12. BEING UNDERFUNDED

Artisans rarely make a bundle. Many struggle even to make a subsistence wage. As Bren Smith pointed out in an op-ed for the *New York Times*:

> The dirty secret of the food movement is that the much-celebrated small-scale farmer isn't making a living. After the tools are put away, we head out to second and third jobs to keep our farms afloat. Ninety-one percent of all farm households rely on multiple sources of income. Health care, paying for our kids' college, preparing for retirement? Not happening.[34]

Eric Glasgow, who runs Grey Barn and Farm, told me that he could not run his farm without external resources. "It's very hard work," he said, "for what amounts to minimum wage."[35]

Glasgow says that Americans are "addicted to cheap food." There are two ways to address this. One is to persuade Americans that cheap food is often bad food. It is processed, adulterated, preserved, and otherwise diminished as a source of nutrition, health, and wellness. Here, at least, we are making real progress. Americans care about wellness. They identify food as a critical part of their pursuit of wellness. They are prepared, some of them, to pay the premiums that attach to good food. Increasingly, those who can buy good food are buying good food.

The other way to address the problem of cheap food is to show that when we pay a premium for good food we are sustaining farms, farmers, farmer's markets, and entire communities.

It turns out that coffeehouses, that other staple of entrepreneurial artisanship, can be problematic in a different way. In an essay for *Slate* titled "Bitter Brew: I Opened a Charming Neighborhood Coffee Shop. Then It Destroyed My Life," Michael Idov gives us an account of the café he opened in New York City:

> The small cafe connects to the fantasy of throwing a perpetual dinner party, and it cuts deeper . . . than any other capitalist urge. To a couple in the throes of the cafe dream, money is almost an afterthought. Which is good, because they're going to lose a lot of it.[36]

The hours can be long and the margins small. And the costs are not just economic but also emotional. Idov says:

> Guess what, dear dreamers? The psychological gap between working in a cafe because it's fun and romantic and doing the exact same thing because you have to is enormous. Within weeks, Lily and I— previously ensconced in an enviably stress-free marriage—were at each other's throats.

This, too, is a question to be addressed through education. Consumers need to understand that when they refuse to buy or, as in this case, refuse to pay, they put at risk the very café that matters so much to their community and their style of life. You can withhold your support from the local café, but this is surely a false economy. You save money but cost yourself the style of life you cherish.

I have written a book on this topic, arguing that various companies and technologies create a "dark value" that does not get reflected in the price of the good or in the mind of the consumer.[37] The artisanal community has a job to do here. Engage in a public education that will help people see what they are getting and what they are supporting when they pay the artisanal premium.

This might be a job for Gwyneth Paltrow, who has turned her brand and TV show into a platform for public education. And she has co-conspirators, including Elise Loehnen:

> Loehnen wasn't just interested in wellness; she was obsessed with it. Wellness, she argued, isn't just about a spa you're going to or a cleanse you've started or a diet you're on. It's how local your food is. It's how the chickens you eat all went to the right schools. It's the water you drink. It's the cures you never thought possible. It's the level of well-being you didn't even know to ask for.[38]

Paltrow and her friends take the broad view. They can see how prices in the market can make (or kill) farms in the countryside. If there is a group capable of communicating the big picture, it's Paltrow and company.

13. STAYING PERSONAL

The artisan undertaking is deeply personal. Mateo Kehler of Jasper Hill Farm puts it this way: "We work on something we love, with people we love, in a place we love."[39]

How different from the person who moves to Los Angeles to work for a record label he doesn't really respect, filled with people he doesn't really like, in a city he loathes . . . but, hey, the money's good and his husband happens to love the city. This sort of thing won't work for the artisan. It's hard to make something matter to the world if it doesn't matter to you.

I remember visiting an IBM office in Armonk, New York. They led me upstairs into the warren of cubicles where the engineers sat. At first I thought I was suffering sudden-onset color blindness. The place was white, from side to side and top to bottom. There wasn't a single thing that differentiated one cubicle from another. Not a single image, memento, personal gesture. No pictures of the family. No drawings from the kids. Just a great, yawning whiteness.

It reminded me a little of the way they used to label offices at Harvard Business School. On your door there was a metal holder. It was designed to hold your business card. You just slide it in. Of course this meant someone (the dean?) could just slide it out. They could erase all evidence of you with the swipe of a wrist.

This sends a message. It says, *You are replaceable. Don't get comfortable. You are a cog in a machine.*

It also says, *Don't take a risk. Don't engage in high-stakes creativity. Don't see if you can reimagine the institution. We are way ahead of you. We can forget you in a second.* When I left HBS, I think a second was actually much more time than they needed.

The artisan, on the other hand, lives in a world that resonates. There's the neighborhood coffee shop where they have your favorite macchiato waiting first thing in the morning. There's the customers who come in first to chat and only then to buy. There are those retailers "who went deep for us" after COVID hit.

But artisans are also in the business of making the world resonate. The conversations over the counter make the world a kinder place for consumers. This is the value add. And this is where the artisan kills P&G, which can make things gleam and work but cannot make them mean, not like this. And this brings us to the next section.

14. PERSONALIZATION

I'm torn. Sometimes I think personalization is pointless. I mean, really, how many differences do we actually need? At one point, Starbucks was claiming that there were eighty-seven thousand combinations at their counter.[40] Surely, that's too many. I'll just have a coffee of the day. (Okay, make it a grande.)

On the other hand, I know people for whom there is only one drink they want from Starbucks, and it's a venti nonfat extra-dry cappuccino. Not somewhat dry. Extra dry, okay?

That's where we are now. We are so accustomed to having things just the way we like them that it feels like the optional is now the necessary. Human beings are noticing machines. We are fantastically good at detecting differences and then coming to rely on them.

Barry Schwartz, professor of social theory and social action at Swarthmore College, thinks this is empty choice. He thinks having so many options is bad for us.[41] But this is what intellectuals always say. Somehow they came to believe that their job is to tell us how bad we have it.[42] (Well, everyone except Steven Pinker.[43]) But the fact of the matter is that choice is gratuitous until we can't imagine the world without it. And if choice was truly a matter that didn't matter, there would be Amazon but no Etsy, Kroger but no farmer's market, Illinois but no Vermont.

Artisanal personalizing creates a lot of value. In the case of Jocelyn Gayle Krodman's Glenda the Fox, it helps me acknowledge, honor, adore my wife. It touches her in a way that no object of mass manufacture could hope to do. I am sure a new car would make a bigger impression. But price is no reflection of value. Glenda the Fox speaks much more powerfully.

Artisans also personalize the point of sale and moment of purchase. When you walk into Darien Cheese, Ken or his wife or another expert behind the counter immediately offers you a piece of cheese. And immediately the "retail encounter" becomes more social and therefore more personal. And this makes the cheese more meaningful. Plus, it's vastly more human.

Consider my usual experience at my local big-box grocery store. I wander around for a while, blinking under the klieg lights. I ask directions from some guy with a badge. He says "far wall" in a way that suggests that he's not completely sure, but that I should understand that he is busy with stuff far more pressing than my need for cheese. Sure enough, it is the far wall. Not the one I thought he meant, of course. But really, there were only four choices and I got lucky on the third try. I cart my plastic packet of Kraft cheese to the checkout and in an outburst of fellow feeling, I say, "Wow, this is a really big store." The woman behind the counter looks at me as if to say, *So go someplace else.* Artisans: 400. Big Box: 0.

Max Weber talked about our efforts to re-enchant the world after science and rationality had managed to make it cold, heartless, and grim.[44] We went back to folklore. We restored magic. We discovered benign forces. We entertained ideas not vouchsafed by science. It wasn't that we wanted to give ourselves over to superstition. But who could live in a world so utterly without warmth, a world so careless of our existence? Almost no one.

Capitalism suffered the same problem, roughly. Big brands were so big, the corporation so heartless, the headquarters, as in the case of P&G, so like an alien spaceship, that they seemed cruel and unreasonable, a punishment. Did they care about us? Care about us? Living way up there in the C-suite, they couldn't even see us. Naturally, they liked to say they cared. Usually in very carefully crafted ads. Every time we turn around some company is saying they're "there for us." *Yeah, right,* we think. No re-enchantment here.

I give you the artisanal revolution. It re-enchanted the world beautifully. All the things we've seen so far, the imperfection, human scale, historical outlook, handmade, raw, all of these helped make the world a kinder, gentler, more intelligible, more habitable place.

I think it's probably fair to say that P&G found this completely bizarre. As nearly as it could tell, the artisan world was bound to fill the world with too many little brands. All that variation and variety. All the barter and swapping. I mean, really, what would Adam Smith say? Well, forget Adam Smith. The real question was for Max Weber, and he would have said, "Good on ya, Tanya," or more deeply learned German words to that effect. For P&G, we could surmise, the artisanal world might as well have been Mars. There wasn't enough water or oxygen to make it profitable or even habitable. For the rest of us, it was just where we wanted to be.

The artisanal revolution helped recover the world we had lost. Yes, thank you, we wanted to see the face of the man who grew our food and shake his hand. It was fun to take the kids out to our CSA farm and introduce them to the patch that would grow their vegetables. On the whole, it was better to deal with someone who knew our names. And, look, knew our tastes so well, he set things aside for our arrival on Saturday morning. Artisans: 600. Big Box: 0.

There's a convention at work in the artisanal world. We always want to trade a few words with our artisan. We're looking for a combination of a little information, emotion, solicitude, and humor. And we always want to end with a laugh. This may be formulaic, but it's a very well-intentioned formula. It's our conventionalized way of saying, *I like you. I admire you. I appreciate you. And I hope that's mutual!*

Mass manufacture delivers the impersonal. Artisans guarantee the personal. The latter is winning. There is something charming about knowing that the Glenda the Fox I may buy for my wife for Christmas is not quite like anything else on the market or even in Jocelyn's studio. It's one of a kind. So, you see, is Pamela. I guess that settles it.[45]

15. PRIVILEGE

Early readers of the manuscript let me have it on the topic of privilege. One of them said:

That busboy working at a restaurant in Midtown Manhattan, the one recently arrived from Nicaragua, he doesn't have any hope of moving out to Hudson, New York, and starting his own start-up. He's hoping to find a way to supplement his minimum-wage salary. And now that he's got a kid on the way, he is staring at the prospect of food insecurity right here in the city.

This is fair. It takes all kinds of capital to be an artisan: intellectual, cultural, economic. We have to have education, a breadth of knowledge and experience, and, most of all, enough money to get started and survive the lean years. So, yes, artisans are creatures of privilege.

On the other hand, most people working as artisans are just scraping by. Many survive with side gigs, second jobs, and living at their parents' home. Compared to some people, they do have advantages. But compared to virtually anyone working in the professional or the creative economy, they are underpaid, overworked, insecure, working without health insurance, and otherwise challenged.

It may have taken privilege to get them here, but it is hard to see them as creatures of privilege now. Indeed, it is probably more sensible and true to see them as people building a way of life a busboy from Nicaragua would welcome. Because this is a diverse community, most artisans are working to reform our culture and our economy. The costs are high, the dangers are high, and the insecurities are high. If this is privilege . . . well, it's not.

And this first community of innovators is helping to create a world that is growing so sufficiently it might someday be able to lower its price points like a drawbridge and admit those who cannot now afford entry. It is probably thanks to the early artisans that so many Americans are prepared to call themselves foodies, and that Walmart and PepsiCo now care about "organic." It is thanks to people like Alice Waters and organizations like Big Green that there are now "learning gardens" where before there were none.

But this pool of enthusiasm isn't quite as broadly distributed as it should be. The artisanal world remains largely the domain of the white and middle-class.

16. INTERSECTIONALITY

There is more to privilege than being white and middle-class. Contemporary culture now acknowledges a profusion of identities, as defined by gender, sex, race, class, age, sexuality, religion, disability, physical appearance. And where these are grounds for prejudice and exclusion (as there often are), we now struggle to take down our prejudices and dismantle exclusion's architecture.

Let's take racism as a case in point. Change here doesn't come merely from, say, persuading colleges to change their admission policies. It doesn't come from people saying they will try to be more sensitive.

The trouble is that racism is a liquid. It finds its way deep into every nook and cranny of our culture. It seeps into our assumptions and our behavior. This means we can't wish it away or will it away. What we need is an exacting study of how racism enters, sometimes invisibly, into the way we think, talk, and act. Only a very concentrated study will help us run this racism to ground. Only exerted effort will allow us to root it out.[46]

This sounds hard, and of course it is. Or, more accurately, it's really uncomfortable. But the good news is that this labor has a reward. As we put old thinking behind us, we can see parts of the world that have been concealed from us, parts of the African-American experience that are astonishing.[47]

Still more illuminating is what happens to American culture when it is more inclusive of African-Americans. As I write this, I know that at the end of the day my wife and I will sit down to watch a TV show called *Bridgerton*. This dramatic series from Netflix makes Georgian England come alive with dramatic and imaginative possibilities that might have impressed even the magnificently gifted Jane Austen. How did this happen? Shonda Rhimes is the show runner. You could argue that Rhimes is one of our modern Jane Austens. She has given us *Grey's Anatomy*, *How to Get Away with Murder*, and *Scandal*. What Rhimes has created is popular culture, to be sure, interesting and accessible to all. But it is also different, richer and more arresting—perhaps due to the fact that Rhimes is African-American. Let's make the artisanal community one of the portals through which African-Americans can fully participate and contribute. It's our job to put down the drawbridge. Worlds will open up: new kinds of culture, new horizons, new partnerships.

Exploring the possibilities.

17. SOCIAL GIFTS, SOCIAL GOODS

Giving is exploding in America. In 2018, people volunteered around 6.9 billion hours of time. As individuals or organizations, Americans gave $410 billion to charity.[48] Even the world of branding and marketing is suddenly all about "purpose." Where once the objective was, frankly, to make as much money as possible, now American corporations want us to know they are committed to creating social good.

Captains of industry and rock stars have been newly generous. Bill Gates, Warren Buffett, and Mark Zuckerberg have all signed a Giving Pledge, committing millions of their personal wealth to philanthropy. But artisanal giving is a finer, more particular affair. When my little town locked down for COVID, suddenly there were little packages every-where, gifts from one household to another. Eggs, honey, bread, jam: gifts without much monetary value. The point was sentimental. Giving a gift says, *I'm thinking of you. I care about you. I hope you're okay.* Connecticut mothers knew that we were in for a long and difficult time. They figured it might take a village after all, and being social felt like an excellent way to get started.

Artisans make gifting easy. Their creations are perfectly gift propor-tioned: authentic, human scale, handmade, they are exactly the right size and shape, plus particular and personal in just the way a gift should be. They are Goldilocks valuable: not too precious, not too mere.

In some artisanal communities, artisanal gifting makes up a big chunk of the gift economy. My respondent in western Massachusetts described the astonishing number of things in motion in her world. One person makes herbal medicine. Someone makes jam. Someone is good with mo-tors. Someone builds websites. And there is so much in motion, people don't need cash. They don't even need markets. Stuff just arrives. Suddenly there's a jar of jam on your doorstep. You don't even have to choose. Your neighbor has raspberry bushes, so you're getting raspberry jam.

This gift exchange is not perfect. Inevitably, someone is giving more than they are getting. Or, much worse, some people are deliberately exploiting the generosity of others. I am thinking of those people who come to a neighborhood café and sit all day, enjoying the free Wi-Fi. They order one cup of coffee. One cup of coffee. (You know who you are. Cut it out.)

All gifting is good, but some of it is expensive. When we give everything, or most everything, away, it is not clear how we sustain ourselves. The intellectuals and academics love these acts of generosity. They see a "gift economy" flourishing. Finally, they say, we have escaped the rigors and asymmetries of capitalism. Now things flow from those who have to those who need.

Moms giving gifts in the COVID era.

I love that idea, of course. I grew up hoping it would be the future. But now that I am a little more worldly, a little more realistic, I take another view. The "gift economy argument" always seems to come from academics who do not actually work for free. In point of fact, they have tenure, fat salaries, job security, and a guaranteed livelihood, no matter how little they work. These are the people who praise others' generosity. I have done ethnographic interviews with teens who make magnificent fan fiction and fan art, all of it for free. "What's that like?" I ask them. The answer is something like, "Hey, I will have to work at McDonald's this summer, because no one is prepared to pay me." And I can't help feeling these artisans have a point. The gift economy works best when people get paid.[49]

18. ARTISANAL ECOSYSTEMS

Some artisans go beyond their own work to create things that help other artisans get in the game and grow. Let's call them ecosystems.

Take the case of Blackberry Farm, a resort hotel and restaurant:

Blackberry Farm is a well-oiled machine when it comes to gathering the requisite ingredients for a full-on foodie experience: teams of gardeners, foragers, brewers, preservationists, and livestock handlers partner with local farmers to generate the decadent final products found in their haute-comfort menus. What's more, they're thrilled to walk you through their meticulous process. There's truly no way to better consume the unpretentious cuisine of the Tennessee Smoky Mountain foothills.[50]

Blackberry Farm is an ecosystem. It encourages local artisans by giving them a place to show their work. It also draws in foodies from national and international communities. Foodies bring in wealth. They take away knowledge.

Raeisha Williams creates an ecosystem too. When Jamar Clark was shot in Minneapolis on November 15, 2015, Williams helped lead a protest. She occupied a police precinct for eighteen days. It was exhausting and absorbing, and afterwards Raeisha wasn't sure what she wanted to do. She had worked on a number of things—helping to run the Minneapolis NAACP, standing for city council, making public service advertising. What was she going to do now?

Williams decided to open the Heritage Tea House in St. Paul. I interviewed her there in early 2019. Heritage is not only a teahouse but also a wine bar and African Heritage boutique. It's styled like a living room. There are photos on the wall that give a glimpse of the history of the local African-American community. One shows a debutante ball from deep in the twentieth century. That woman there in a row of debutantes? The one on the far left? That's Raeisha's grandmother, looking a little unimpressed by the occasion but holding the red ribbon.

We did our interview in the Tea House. There were people coming and going, eager for Raeisha's attention. It's hard not to be. She is, apparently, lit from within. Raeisha told me Heritage was designed to welcome everyone: activists, foodies, anthropologists. She means to empower people and create community. It's a kind of "come for the tea, stay for the revolution" thing. The mayor drops by. Politicians and community leaders turn up.

Raeisha has curatorial abilities. She is using her teahouse and her natural incandescence to collect people and combine them.[51]

Heritage reminded me of Rao's, an Italian restaurant in Spanish Harlem. This, too, is a place where people network. You can tell by the way they're dressed. At one table there is a woman who looks like she might be a politician. Her outfit is expensive, fashionable. She is eating with someone who looks like he might be a Teamster. His outfit is expensive but not fashionable. At another table, there's a guy in a suit eating with a guy in a tracksuit (and wearing a really expensive Rolex). These are people from different parts of New York City. Rao's is one of the places they can "find" one another.

Minneapolis has always been a diverse community too. Heritage can help bring some of its various parties together. But the city is struggling to manage its diversity. And then there's the sense, recently, that this is a city on the precipice of civic disorder, since the killing of George Floyd launched a nationwide flood of protests. Now it's really essential for someone to stage a space where people can find one another. Heritage can help there too. As a curator and connector, Raeisha has a role to play.[52]

Consider Mateo Kehler and his brother Andy, who together founded and run Jasper Hill Farm in Greensboro, a town of 706 people in northern Vermont. I spent an hour on the phone with Mateo and I was wowed. It's hard to tell whether Jasper Hill is an economic enterprise embedded in a social objective or the other way around. Business and culture intertwine seamlessly.

Mateo is interested in the transfer of wealth. He believes that economic practice and government policy have hollowed out rural communities, moving money from rural America to big cities, from agriculture and industry into financial services. Mateo's idea is to use Jasper Hill Farm to make wealth run in the other direction. Urban dwellers with plenty of disposable income happen to love his cheese, and they are prepared to pay handsomely for it. And when they do, capital flows back to rural Vermont. This is Jasper Hill as a force for good. This is artisanal economy as a way to address a pressing social need.

Jasper Hill is so well known in the foodie world that it draws many visitors each year for tours . . . or just to stand in awe of what the Kehler brothers have accomplished. If Jasper Hill were a conventional money-making operation, it would have a company store to capture revenue from all those visitors.

But Mateo and his brother decided against this. Instead, they reached out to Willey's, the general store in Greensboro, and made it their unofficial "company store." This gives the general store an extra $100,000 a year in revenue, no small thing in a town of fewer than a thousand people. Mateo says it felt like the right thing to do, because Willey's is a venerated local institution, family owned and operated for five generations. If Jasper Hill could help Willey's, the Kehler brothers felt they had to try. As Mateo put it, "We don't want to compete with them. They are such an important part of life here." Imagine how much could change if Walmart thought like this.

Sarah Lagrotteria and Tricia Wheeler have created Flowers & Bread, which they describe as "a multi-dimensional space that houses an elegant café, a recreational learning space, and is a place to engage your hands in the old-world traditions of bread baking, floral arranging, and cooking from a wood-fired oven."[53] As ecosystems go, this may be the most beautiful of all.

Frank Giustra is the publisher of *Modern Farmer*. He launched the Million Gardens Movement to respond to the effects of the COVID crisis, including "social isolation, disrupted supply chains and economic hardship." As he said, "simply growing a tomato can be an act of hope and resilience that unites us."[54] The Million Gardens Movement website gives instruction on how to create herb spirals, dwarf fruit trees, worm composting, and other acts of pandemic gardening. The idea is to help gardens bloom in backyards, in community plots, on balconies and fire escapes, then help distribute this bounty from those who have to those who need. The hope is that if we can make gardens bloom, we can make food deserts bloom. If we make food deserts and diverse gardens bloom, we have literally made a common ground for a varied America.[55]

Tyson Gersh, co-founder and executive director of the Michigan Urban Farming Initiative, has recovered tracts in a once intensely urban Detroit, returning it to farmable land. In the process he has hosted over 10,000 volunteers in over 100,000 hours of volunteer service, grown over 80,000 pounds of over 300 varieties of produce, which has been distributed to over 2,500 households within two square miles of MUFI's headquartered space, formed numerous partnerships with global brands (i.e., BASF, the Scotts-MiracleGro Company, General Motors, et cetera), and orchestrated over 3.5 million dollars' worth of residential investment.[56]

When artisans build ecosystems, they must contend with political issues that wouldn't necessarily come up had they stuck to a freestanding enterprise. Thus, Tyson Gersh is sometimes accused of "neocolonialism," because some perceive him as more interested in developing neighborhoods than supplying cheaper (or free) produce for food deserts. The larger the ecosystem, the bigger the systemic effects, and the more likely it is that political differences of some kind will emerge.[57]

Some ecosystems are designed to enable other artisans or even civilians. In the first case, we craft a space in which would-be or early-stage artisans assemble to think about what they might want to do in a full-blown artisanal enterprise. We could think of this as a lab, a place of exploration and experimentation, where people can look for options and see what speaks to them most powerfully.

In the second case, the civilian case, what we are doing is setting up a place where people can throw their own pots or even make their own bubble gum. A recent experiment from London: "Artisan is the world's first gum micro-factory, where Joe Public can hand make tiny batches of oral fixation in any flavour he likes—the three-year dream of jellymongers Bompas & Parr."[58]

One of the ecosystems that matters most is the one created by the archivists, curators, chroniclers, and documentarians. So much of the artisan world springs up unexpectedly. It is an act of ingenuity that is not anticipated by the artisanal "handbook." (Naturally, there isn't a handbook.) And so much of what happens is evanescent. It's there at one fair and gone the next.

So the artisanal movement needs chroniclers, both to look backwards and to give the movement the chance to see forward. Perhaps the most remarkable example here is the work of Faythe Levine, who, with her partner Cortney Heimerl, has created a book and a documentary called *Handmade Nation*.[59] These give us a window on artisanal ideas and practice. Research began for Levine in 2006, and it would take her nineteen thousand miles and trips to fifteen cities to complete. The anthropologist in me tips its hat to the artisan in her.

What Levine has constructed is an ecosystem of knowledge and understanding. Here's how she sees it:

> We are celebrating a generation of makers. We are reshaping how people consume and interpret the handmade. I want to remind people that craft is what you make it. *Handmade Nation* attempts to capture what is happening in this amazing community, of which I consider myself a part. It is a labor of love, appreciation, and respect. Our community is just beginning to grow into our roles of knitter, book binder, shoemaker, painter, seamstress, potter, etc. We appreciate the generations of makers who came before us and from whom we draw inspiration and support. In turn, we are setting the groundwork for future generations, leading by example and showing the creative paths you can take.[60]

Perfect.

Perhaps the most powerful ecosystem in the artisanal world is the craft fair. Not so long ago, as Susan Beal notes, people gathered at local church bazaars. From those modest beginnings, any event can attract hundreds of vendors and thousands of attendees.[61] The Bazaar Bizarre started in Boston in 2001. The first Renegade Craft Fair started in Chicago in 2003. Stitch Austin was founded in 2003. Faythe Levine started the Art vs. Craft fair in Milwaukee in 2004.

The Renegade Craft Fair was organized by Sue Blatt and Kathleen Habbley, who, in the fearless spirit of DIY, noticed that there wasn't yet a national fair for the new crafting scene."[62] Christy Petterson met with Shannon Mulkey and Susan Voelker to consider what they could do in Atlanta. They came up with the name Indie Craft Experience and a mission: "a summertime event that would include a craft market, fashion show, live music, charity raffle, art show and a guaranteed good time."[63]

These events are hothouses for the artisanal movement. Each one demonstrates a new set of possibilities. The displays instantaneously inspire attendees, who return the following year with creative proposals of their own. And there is a relentless recruitment going on. People come one year as observers, the next year as consumers, and the year after that as artisans. All of this creativity and community begins to generate more and more proceeds. Thus does this ecosystem help supply the precious profits on which the larger ecosystem eventually depends.

19. BEING ANTI—ADAM (SMITH)

Almost all the things we've seen that define the artisan, the imperfection, human scale, handmade products, rawness, localism, being historical, staying unbranded, personal, and personalized, and social gifts and goods and ecosystems, put the artisan more or less at odds with the capitalism of contemporary culture.

The chief cause of this opposition is that artisans prefer to see and to put their economic activity in a larger context. This can be a social, cultural, ethical, ecological, artistic context. But one way or another, the artisanal economy is embedded in a larger world, from which it draws and to which it gives. How the artisan embeds her enterprise is up to her.[64]

There are a bundle of additional differences we should touch on briefly.

19.1: The artisan world is more about the producer than the consumer. In the old-fashioned, twentieth-century scheme of things, the point of the enterprising enterprise was to know the consumer. In the words of Charles Coolidge Parlin in 1912, the consumer was king.[65] This meant putting the consumer at the center of things.

Artisan consumers aren't kings. They aren't even courtiers. Sure, they are consulted. They are treated as collaborators. But they are no longer kings.

This reversal of fortune is due to several things and especially the influence of Steve Jobs, who believed that consumers couldn't know what they wanted until he made it for them. Alice Waters also made a contribution here. In the words of Thomas McNamee: "She alone would dictate how every dish was to be prepared, down to the finest touch of technique: how brown a particular sauté should be, how many shallots to sweeten a sauce, how finely chopped. She knew exactly how she wanted everything to taste, to look, to smell, to feel."[66]

Artisanal producers tend to know more and better than consumers. We could send a dish back at Chez Panisse . . . well, no, on second thought, we probably wouldn't. We take for granted that Alice Waters knows more and better than we do.

Artisans are revered in their local communities and even on the national stage. (This is true, as we have seen of Ken and Drew. And this can be a problem for the artisan. Erin told me she feared being seen as someone special.)[67] The downside here is the artisan who comes to think too well of himself.

19.2: Capitalism lives to optimize. Making the most broadly appealing product for the largest audience in the cheapest way, this was the path to profit. The artisan is inclined to make the product she thinks is most compelling, for a small audience, not with the cheapest method, but the most crafted one. This is the artisanal difference.

19.3: Capitalism is prepared to create what it calls externalities. These are the unintended consequences: smokestacks throwing off pollution, effluent piped into nearby streams. Once it's off the grounds of the corporation, well, it's someone else's problem.

But artisans take responsibility for things that come from them. They mop up after themselves. Conventional businesses are happy to throw things "away." Artisans believe (correctly) that there is no "away" on spaceship Earth.

19.4: Artisans prefer intrinsic benefits over extrinsic ones. This distinguishes them from most people who "work for a living." Those people work for a paycheck. They are paid whatever someone prefers to pay them.

Artisans hope to "make a living" from their craft. But they are also paid richly in intrinsic benefits. There is the joy, the pleasure, the satisfaction, of doing something difficult well. Relatively few run a dry-cleaning operation for the satisfaction. They do it to make a wage and support their family. Everyone who is making chocolate, baking bread, or running a coffee shop has higher aspirations. They have committed to a craft and this craft pays them in pleasure however much (or little) it pays them in cash. The dry cleaner is "in it for the money," we say. Why else would he do something like this? Artisans have an additional set of rewards.

19.5: Artisans are sensitive to a bigger picture that captures not just natural externalities, but a broader range of things. The earliest expression of this was perhaps the button created by Stuart Brand, the one that read: "Why haven't we seen a photograph of the whole Earth yet?"

Artisans take for granted that beyond their immediate concern are entire domains that need discovery and examination. They are more inclined to ask, about their own enterprises and others, "What does this coffee shop have to do with the community in which we find ourselves?" It's a sense of diligence, and mindfulness. It is precisely this kind of question that leads to the creation of slam poetry evenings and community events. Tyler Florence started to think about the farm from which his food came. Artisans spend a lot of time casting the net wide.

19.6: Artisans like transparency. They believe that they should be able to see the full supply chain, and so should the consumer. If there are people laboring in the kitchen or on the assembly line, we should be able to glimpse the conditions that govern their labor. There is no backstage or behind the scenes. It is, or ought to be, visible to all.

In a sense, transparency is what the artisan has in lieu of a brand: *Look into us and judge what you see there. See into our hearts; detect what you can there. This is who we are.*

19.7: The artisanal world was an obscure enthusiasm for a relatively tiny world for most of the twentieth century, and it is now growing sufficiently to make a substantial place for itself in the world. As it grows it is in a position to recruit more widely.

The artisanal approach stands as a way to solve some of the problems created by the new economic realities of the twenty-first century. It can be a source of employment for the millions of people who can no longer realistically hope for industrial jobs. Too often people respond to their loss of permanent industrial employment with desperate measures. Social pathologies blossom. The artisanal economy is a source of employment but also community and stability. Politicians and policy makers can harness the artisanal disruption for policy purposes and social good.

Besides which, there are 92 million boomers now undergoing, or contemplating, a shift from their working lives into something called retirement. Thanks to research I did for the Canadian Heart and Stroke Foundation, I know that plenty of boomers are healthy and wealthy enough to take a new approach. They refuse the traditional strategy of "scaling down" as timid and defeatist. What they want is a qualitative change to how they live. For this group, "going artisanal" is a plausible next step.

Recruiting should happen most surely among millennials and Gen Zers, for whom the artisanal movement can be a source of inspiration as well as a new economic narrative. These generations believe in social purpose and social entrepreneurship. On the whole, boomers ask capitalism to create economic value. Younger generations demand that it also creates social value. Nothing produces social values more surely than the artisanal economy. (Not even all those big brands newly touting purpose.)

Recruitment for the artisan movement comes from robots. At first we thought robots would simply take over manual and menial labor. Now we see they can take over white-collar and creative work as well. The financial advice community is being hollowed out as I write this. The economist Tyler Cowen thinks we might be able to see a future that contains "a permanent class of long-term unemployed, who probably can't be helped much by monetary and fiscal policy."[68]

Americans will not tolerate a set of values that finds them wanting. They simply make a virtue of their necessity. In the present case, this means that Americans will find a way of living that forgives them their unemployment and that suggests a better way of living in the world. The handiest, most compelling narrative for them to employ is the artisanal one. We might see large numbers of people living in rural, barter communities—stepping out of, and happily away from, the mainstream.

If robots recruit for the artisanal revolution, it may prove COVID does too. As I write this, we find ourselves living in the remains of a once-robust economy. The need to protect ourselves from COVID infection has forced the closure of restaurants, theaters, and businesses of all kinds. It is possible that this economy will be slow to return to vibrancy. The real fear is that it might prove to be caught in a downward cycle, from which recovery is painfully slow. As it stands, people are wondering if New York City will ever recover its former prosperity. A diminished New York City would represent a terrible wound for the rest of the nation.

A national economic downturn would create vast unemployment. And this unemployment would inflict on an entire nation the kind of hardships we have seen in the deindustrialized Midwest. In some communities there, meth production was one of the few vital parts of the economy. And meth consumption was a temptation many found impossible to resist.[69] When unemployment and addiction are your alternatives, the artisanal economy may well prove to be the most appealing "life alternative" for many.

19.8: And the money is sometimes a problem.

We know from the story of Portland's Stumptown Coffee that things can get rocky when the artisan sells out. Stumptown sold a piece of the company to private equity firm TSG Consumer Partners. There was what Ryan Tate calls a "massive blowback from indie coffee fans," with criticism from Todd Carmichael at Esquire (which asked readers to "vote with your dollar and avoid Wall Street–owned roasters") and Ruth Brown at *Willamette Week*.[70]

So there is capital, and capital. When the financial support comes from friends, and relatives, that's one thing. When it comes from local investors, that, too, is "okay." But when it comes from "Wall Street," there is a feeling, apparently, that a fox has been invited into the henhouse. The artisan needs to think hard about where her financial support comes from and whether she wishes to pay the hidden costs attached.[71]

19.9: For the artisan, it's rarely about the image. While some artisans have celebrity thrust upon them, most are prepared to work in relative, if not outright, obscurity. This is noble. It may also be unwise. Yes, we are a celebrity culture. Yes, American capitalism is preoccupied with selling images sometimes more than reality. But it may be wrong for artisans to be so camera shy, so humble. (You are hearing this from a Canadian, so take note.)

Currently, we have a continuum—on one end, the artisan as a self-adoring celebrity, and at the other, the artisan as too modest for his own good. The reader must choose. Personally, I think this calls for a trade-off. I think the artisan wants enough celebrity to aid with sales, marketing, and fundraising, but not so much that a cult of personality threatens to interfere with ego or business.

19.10: There are mysteries at work in the world of the artisan. They remind me of a famous conversation previously mentioned between two transcendentalists living in Concord, Massachusetts, in the nineteenth century. One says to the other that he's seen a young man sitting on a path examining a frog. The second man says, "Surely, that's not very odd." The first man replies, approvingly, "Yes, but he was still there when I walked past him five hours later."[72]

There is an interest in the thingness and treating this thingness as a portal to ways of thinking and feeling. Working with our hands, in a material, on an object, this can prompt us to leave the here and now and squeeze into other ways of thinking. I touched on this when I talked about flow.

Mind you, some things in the artisanal gift are mysterious for not very mysterious reasons. Bees, for instance. One of my respondents installed beehives in her backyard during COVID. She loved them: "It's like having an ancient court in your garden." This court has inspired a literature and a scholarship: "You can read everything that's interesting about chickens in one night. . . . But you can read about bees every night for the rest of your life."[73]

19.11: The artisan world has a certain ambivalence for design and fashion. Some feel these are wrong for the artisan. Surely, they are too exuberant, playful, governed by change. Artisans are about verities that endure. Fashion is too artificial, and governed by wizards in Paris and Rome. Shouldn't everything artisanal be more grounded, more sincere, less given to artifice?

But the owners of Arethusa Farm in Litchfield, Connecticut, George Malkemus and Tony Yurgaitis were, until last year, president and vice president of the shoe company Manolo Blahnik USA. Their dairy is widely praised, and they make an organic, artisanal, hand-packed ice cream that is prized across the U.S.

Yurgaitis feels no ambivalence:

> People sometimes think there are two totally separate things that we
> do—our shoe business and the farm—but we approach everything
> the same way. We have a certain style of making it what we want it
> to be.[74]

For Yurgaitis, fashion wins the tug-of-war. But for many artisans, anything that looks even vaguely fashionable feels a bit iffy. Fashion feels like something at odds with the artisan's sincerity, her authenticity. After all, fashion changes often and eagerly. For the artisan, this feels wrong. Surely, the things that matter are grounded in tradition and enduring over time.

But every artisan will find the useful compromise and his own place on the continuum.

19.12: Trends are a mixed blessing for the artisan. On the one hand, it was as a trend that the artisanal revolution came up to displace industrial food. It was as a trend that the artisanal revolution ran through American food, recruiting millions of supporters and participants.

But what trends bring in they can also take away. The artisan lives in a culture transformed by a series of cultural disruptions, one hot on the heels of the next. Whether we like it or not, the artisan lives within fashion's sphere of influence. At the moment, the artisanal is fashionable. That could change. This much is inescapable: the artisanal came up as a trend. It, too, may pass. No trend is forever.

Indeed, there could be evidence that a counterreformation has been underway for some time. The engines of satire and ridicule are loud. Ten years ago, David Rees presented himself in a pious video as the "artisanal pencil sharpener." Sitting in a white shirt and a black apron, Rees gives a completely humorless account of sharpening pencils. The advice is practical and philosophical: "It is possible to sharpen a pencil without a pencil sharpener, but it is impossible to sharpen a pencil without a pencil."[75] This point has troubled deep thinkers for centuries. Now we know.

Paul Riccio gives us a mockumentary treatment of the Timmy brothers, two guys who make "bespoke, artisanal water." Riccio's inspiration is Christopher Guest's mockumentary *This Is Spinal Tap*. His execution is excellent. Terry Timmy intones, "I know what wetness is for me, but what is that for you? It could be something completely different."[76]

McDonald's UK has done an ad ridiculing the shortcomings of artisanal coffee: the prices are too high, the hours too short, the menu too complicated, the wait too long, and the barista is so much cooler than we are.[77]

Lewis Black used an appearance on *The Daily Show* to ridicule the very notion of the artisanal: "Snapper, tilapia, who gives a shit? That's what the ketchup's for."[78] Somewhat less shouty treatment comes from Fred Armisen and Carrie Brownstein, who in a *Portlandia* skit give us a couple who cannot proceed with their restaurant meal unless they have all the necessary artisanal reassurances. Carrie wants to know if the chicken is USDA organic, Oregon organic, or just Portland organic? Fred asks whether the chicken is local. He then asks if the chicken's food was local.

Just who was the chicken, anyhow? Fred and Carrie learn the chicken's name was Colin.[79]

All of this is good fun until someone forces a change in our culture. And that could happen. Wave after wave of satire and ridicule could make us tire of the artisanal movement. What if it dropped into the trough where all popular things go when they suddenly lose their first glow of celebrity? And, as we have seen, there is enough here to work with, when the repudiating mood comes upon us. The artisanal thing can be pretentious, humorless, silly, and self-indulgent. Some of the people who work the counter of the artisan world appear to pay themselves in self-regard. They punish any consumer who's unworthy of the good they are buying. Artisans live in a glass house.

All things come in on a trend. Most of them are eventually swept away by the next new thing. A few lucky ones get to stay on. Actually, they build in. They become a fixed and standard part of our world, relatively safe from removal. It's too early to say which kind of trend the artisanal is, passing or permanent. Chances are it's the latter, but the artisan must remain alert to the possibility that the earth is moving beneath their feet. Watch for the new.

19.13: The last piece of our anti–Adam Smith character is authenticity. The trouble is it's often easier to detect the authentic than define it. We have noted the things that signal the authentic, that help build it up, the imperfect, a human scale, being handmade, rawness, localism, happiness, being historical, unbranded, underfunded, personal, personalized, committed to social gifts and social goods, constructive of (or at least participating in) ecosystems, and other anti-Smith properties. But some of these can be missing and we still say that something is entirely authentic.

At a minimum, the artisan is not "in it for the money." She is more interested in the relationship than the transaction. She is driven by a larger purpose. She aims to create something useful in the world, valuable for the community, and sustainable for the planet. Perhaps the key is no fakery, no fronting, no manufacturing impressions. (These, too, should be made by hand.) What you see ought to be what you get.

20. SIMPLIFYING

One virtue of an artisan approach to life is that it's radically simplifying. It looks at the great profusion of contemporary life, the multitude of ways of being, acting, dressing, living, and opts for a reduced set: the artisanal option.

I found this out the hard way when attending the Basilica Farm & Flea Market in Hudson, New York, a couple of years ago. I was there with my friend Peter Spear, and we were surveying the crowd, hundreds of people crammed into a small space: talking, selling, shopping.

Peter asked, "How are you feeling about your coat?"

I looked at him with surprise and said, "Er, fine, I guess. Why, what's wrong with it?"

He said, "Look around."

What I saw were people dressed in autumnal colors, flat greens, dull blues, dark reds, lots of subtly different browns. Me, I was wearing a bright yellow jacket. I think I got it from L.L.Bean or someplace. They call it a squall jacket, I think. You see a lot of them in New England. I wear mine in the hope that I will not get run over while out walking at night. But here in Hudson, what it said was, *I own a boat. You, probably, do not.* I was conspicuous. I was showy.

Artisans are not showy. They do not make a spectacle of their wealth or their social standing. In fact, generally speaking, they care little for wealth or social standing. Artisans live modestly. They don't own a car if they can manage without one. When they do own a car, it's more likely to be a Subaru than a luxury sedan. Their clothing isn't fashionable. Artisans don't buy multiples. They don't build walk-in closets. They don't renovate their homes for show. Their American dream is not sumptuous. Their idea of the "good life" is "simpler is better."[80]

This is all good. But it's not without a problem. With simplification, we run the risk of making the palette too small and too rigid. Sometimes you want a yellow jacket in the midst of all those autumnal colors. Not nautical yellow. No, I just looked like an idiot. But a non-autumnal yellow, just to mix things up. We need noise in the signal. We need things that are slightly off course and out of step. Otherwise, we end up looking like Canada, a place where conformity rules some people so completely it extinguishes the very creativity that makes a country live.

Variety is our fellow traveler. Well before the artisanal trend beat its way in from the margin, variety was putting itself at the center of things. We were a mass culture, with mass marketing, mass media, and mass consumption. Variety was unusual, exotic even. Then it took over popular culture, exploding especially in the 1990s. There it was in poetry collections, street fashion, music.[81]

This is when a culture loses its centers. When elites lose their grip. When hierarchies collapse. When distinctions get muddled (in a good way). This is when variety becomes diversity. There are just so many people inventing so much culture from so many diverse points of view that we can no longer police our culture—including some, excluding others. We have broken down the hegemony that says, *Here's how you must make a poem, a TV show, or an argument.* Now everyone is welcome to the party. There are bright jackets everywhere.

That leaves us with a tension. The artisanal community is a respite precisely in that it allows us to take refuge from the blooming, buzzing world out there. It speaks to us precisely because it is not distracted and complicated by a hundred points of view. The artisanal world has a certain constancy, clarity, and simplicity.

All good. But we mustn't allow ourselves to be terrorized by this constancy. We need to let things in. We can't shut ourselves off from what contemporary culture has managed to open up. Or, to put this somewhat more grandly, we can't allow our repudiation of the city to alienate us from the vigors and virtues of city life.

Aristotle praised the city for its ability to bring together people who are dissimilar.[82] The great English critic Isaiah Berlin picked up the theme:

> It is hardly possible to overrate the value . . . of placing human beings in contact with persons dissimilar to themselves, and with modes of thought and action unlike those with which they are familiar.[83]

We can't let our simplicity shut us out of this.

21. CREATIVITY

Creativity is a terrible houseguest. It doesn't care that you have a routine, that you have made this place "just the way you like it." Creativity likes to do things its way. It prefers to turn things upside down. It doesn't do anything as grand (or fashionable) as "resist" and "disrupt." It's not deeply unhappy with the existing order of things. It just doesn't care. It always has another idea, even if it's a minor one. Creativity is always waving its hand, demanding our attention. It's always asking, *Okay, sure, I know you do it that way, but what about this?*

Creativity is a wellspring of the novelty that is increasingly our best method of adaptation. The world moves quickly. The Heraclitean stream is now a torrent. And nothing is exempt from change. Heraclitus had a phrase for it: "panta rhei" (everything flows).[84] Surely, one of the best ways to stay in touch with this change is to give our creativity free rein. It is capable of running out ahead of what we are thinking now, consorting and cavorting with new ideas and impulses. Then it returns to us, bearing gifts and provocations.

This is good for the artisan. She loves creativity. But it's also bad. After all, the artisan is committed to the historical, the continuous, the conventional. She embraces continuities that run back hundreds of years. The movement is to some extent a bulwark against the raging torrent of change that now consumes us. The artisan says, in effect, *What if we posit these few things, devote ourselves to them, perfect them, and return to them? What if we stand for continuity?*

This is good and a powerful position to take, but it puts us at a disadvantage. Anyone who wants to participate in American culture needs to know that culture. It is one thing to refuse that constant, mindless fizz of this culture. It is another to lose touch with its center of gravity, which moves inexorably, stranding those who don't move too.

We need a creativity that makes us uncomfortable, that moves away from what we know, that leads us toward something new. The fact that it makes us uncomfortable is a good thing. That's the sound of our boundaries being stretched, our options being multiplied. Artisans can't be all convention and tradition. That way lies stasis and orthodoxy.

22. UNEMPLOYMENT KILLING

The scourge of unemployment is upon us. It was once assumed that hard work and an education guaranteed a good job and the ability to make enough money to raise a family and make a place for ourselves in the world. This American dream is now fading for millions of Americans as they see jobs being shipped off to China, Canada, Mexico, and across the Third World even as they are preempted by the rise of the robotization of work.

For many Americans, this means the job they have just lost in the industrial economy may be the last such job they will ever hold. Bad things happen when people are pushed out of the industrial economy. Despair grows. Drugs beckon. Families suffer. Communities descend into chaos. Lives fall apart.[85]

And that's where the artisanal economy can help. It has several excellent properties as a substitute for industrial work. It is compact enough that it can be staged in our own home, and if we are lucky enough to have our own house now we have something really useful to do in that backyard.

It doesn't take a lot of money. It doesn't take a lot of learning. We can start small and bootstrap our way to something larger. Plus, we can eat (or wear or share) our surplus.

But this is where I think it can really serve us. To engage in artisanal labor is to regain control of some part of your own destiny. You don't have to wait for a factory to move back into town.

I did an interview with a guy who keeps bees in the backyard of his home in suburban New Jersey.[86] He had 6 hives. He estimates that he produces 45 pounds of honey a year and at $8 a pound that's around $3,000. To be sure, hives, equipment, and bees are not inexpensive. But even relatively small amounts can make a big difference.

In addition to the financial benefits, there are other values. The beekeeper has something to trade with neighbors, a way to fight the damage done by colony collapse disorder. And as we noted earlier, there are poetic benefits: those bees in the garden are an ancient court with their own rituals and mysteries.

Perhaps the best thing about an artisanal approach is that it gives the individual and his community a chance to build something that is more fulfilling, humane, connected, and connecting than the jobs it seeks to replace. And it doesn't take a project flown in from Washington, dreamed up by a contingent from MIT, or a reparative grant pried away from the Sackler family.[87] A community can make its own way.

23. ARKISHNESS

I met a guy driving for Uber. We got talking. (The anthropologist wants to hear anything you want to tell him. Okay, almost anything.)

He was talking about the business he used to have. He had been making iPad stands out of wood. And it went pretty well, he said. The stands were beautiful to look at. People liked them. Then our conversation petered out.

"What happened?" I asked.

He said, "I could never get the marketing right. I just didn't get it."

Wow, I thought, *of all the things to be bad at! Marketing!* It's not rocket science. This guy had done the artisanal thing with the hand, head, and heart. He had mastered human scale, the imperfect, the local, the historical, and the personal. But to stumble on marketing, what should be the easy stuff—what a shame.

I talked to another artisan who failed because he just couldn't get the hang of social media. And I guess I can see that Twitter and Facebook can be a little intimidating. Wait, no, I can't. They are harder than marketing, especially if you come from a pre-digital generation. On the other hand, you only need sustain the discomfort of not knowing for a little while and then you've got it. There are no mysteries in social media that can't be extinguished by a short course on YouTube. And it's not optional. For an artisan not to use social media inflicts a mortal wound.

The artisan must be an ark. The challenge is to master not only your craft but all the other things required to run a business. How to work a spreadsheet. How to do marketing. How to do social media. How to do sales. How to manage customers. How to chat people up at a farmer's market. How to do supply chain marketing. How to do PR, HR, and stakeholder management. Happily, cultivating range of this kind is the latest thing.[88]

And most of this will be self-taught. There are programs emerging. Under the guidance of Namita Wiggers, Warren Wilson College has developed a Master of Arts in Critical Craft Studies.[89] This is "the first program of its kind to integrate American studies, anthropology, art history, decorative art history, design history, social history, and material and visual culture studies." There are many practical courses of study online. I looked for a network that allows artisans to exchange knowledge. This is the traditional means of artisan education. But I couldn't find anything particularly robust. Please, will someone build one of these, a LinkedIn for artisans?

It's also possible to buy marketing, bookkeeping, and design services and advice online from the likes of Upwork and Fiverr.

For better or worse, the artisan is obliged to be freestanding and self-directing. There is no company to confine her. But this also means there is no company to sustain her.

24. A DOME ABOVE, A GRID BELOW

I sit pondering. I have two cats on my desk. This leaves me one short of my minimum. I can't really manage without the entire crew: Molly, Vivienne, and Zsa Zsa. (That's Zsa Zsa on the right. She's asleep on her feet. Vivienne is about to follow suit. I don't know where Molly is. TikTok keeps her pretty busy.)

I was thinking about Kentucky, where people were giving generously without being able to say why or to whom the gift was going. Pressed, they would say "oh, Kentucky," "the church," "the neighborhood," "my family," "the planet," "young men struggling," or "old guys lying." There were lots of beneficiaries, but no real plan.

The author and his sleepy assistants.

Clearly, Kentuckians weren't keeping careful track. They were throwing off good, and they were doing it recklessly, generously. I could see the same thing happening everywhere we did research, Connecticut, Iowa, New York State, Washington State, New Jersey, Michigan, and California. Domes up there in the air. Filling with generosity. Drawn upon by everyone and especially those in need.

But there is another way to think about the artisan. And that's someone who also lives in a grid. Kaelin and Heather Vernon raising Leicester longwool sheep at Peacefield Farms in Kentucky are constantly sharing with and caring for their neighbors. But ultimately, they are freestanding. They are individuated. They are separate. There's a group of flower farmers in Northern California. Originally, they hoped to create a collective,

but for a variety of reasons that didn't quite work out. Yes, they still coop-
erate and collaborate, but at the end of the day they, too, are freestanding.

And this is when a picture began to form in my head. There's a dome
above and a grid below. The dome fills with goodness. The grid defines
difference. The two work together. Acts of generosity rise to fill the dome.
Much of what is actual and practical, that helps make the grid.

There is a tension between dome and grid. The dome is beguiling. A
community can feel itself creating good and giving it away. People don't
keep track. They don't claim credit. No one knows how much there is
or what its overall effect must be. Surely, some say, we are a collective. We
have built a common good.

The temptation is to say, *All right, then. That dome is our collective.* But
the moment we try to keep track, or apportion credit, things get tricky.
Some people seem to give so much more than others. And there are so
many kinds of goods in circulation, the act of measurement is impossible.
Rules emerge. And fail. Schemes are crafted. And fail. Figuring out what
each of us owes to others and then extracting and distributing it . . . we
struggle. We fail.

We would very much like to relocate the whole of the artisanal
world in the dome. This is, we want to say, our accomplishment, where
we share our abilities and take for our needs. Surely, someone somewhere
has made this work. But not us. Failing is the easy part. We have spent
entire decades refining and perfecting our failure. It's now indubitable.

And that leaves us inclined to return to a grid. This is the world
where everyone assumes responsibility for their own enterprise. Then
they don't need to rely on others. And now they can give freely without
worrying about whether the Kombucha brothers are more or less generous than the Top Crops family. Everyone just gives. We'll be fine. Exacting
and tracking, that's so very joyless. Just give. Our generosity is reckless for
a reason.

Most artisans have both dome and grid "in their blood." Take the case of Thomas Massie. He went off to MIT and could have just kept going. But he returned to serve Kentucky. Why? Well, dome. That's why. People feel tattooed from the inside. And most of them come home. But when Massie came back to Kentucky, he built himself a self-sufficient farm on a distant hillside well away from other Kentuckians. Lots of artisans seem to share this distinction. They are both freestanding and part of something larger.

Dome above and grid below is one of the organizing principles of the artisan's world. It means everyone is called upon to make a simple distinction. What do they owe the "dome"? What must they do for the "grid"? It also helps as a warning to the newcomer. Don't join the artisanal world if you expect only to "dome." Don't join the artisanal world, if you expect only to "grid." We need you to be both generous and responsible.

We are a culture that is rethinking its individualism. We used to encourage individuals to individuate, to define themselves as separate, to mark themselves as different, to show themselves as special. Now we are searching for a way to acknowledge and reinforce our connectedness.

Competition is diminished. Status matters less. Conspicuous consumption begins to look merely odd. Luxury goods look vulgar and overweening. The status hierarchy becomes the preoccupation of a few. In the unflinching gaze of the social scientist, we have always been embedded in a whole, less freestanding than we wanted to think. But now Americans are catching up to the scientist. We see ourselves as embedded too.[90]

So the artisanal movement, by combining dome and grid, manages to capture both faces of America: our emerging collectivity, our enduring individualism. This is good news. When cultural movements capture diverse trends within American culture, they flourish.

6

THE MOMENT

CRAFT IN THE TIME OF COVID

ARTISANS BEFORE COVID

In August of 2008, Epson introduced a new line of printers.[1] They claimed it set "new standards in image customization and quality." They called it their "Artisan line." The response was overwhelming. One could hear the nation saying, "Artisan printers? Oh, please, that is so dumb."

But even boneheaded marketing can signal something. Apparently, the artisan idea was now so far above the novelty horizon that it was visible even to the people who made printers, and so resonant in our culture that it was useful even to those who sold them.

Alice Waters ignited her part of the revolution with the founding of Chez Panisse in 1971. Her diaspora of chefs then spilled across America, all those charismatic men and women, dropping by tables at their restaurants to press the flesh and baptize the novitiate. Lo! Patrons were now foodies, and these foodies made a second, larger diaspora, leaving restaurants to create new diets for their kids. For over thirty years, the artisan idea was the little engine that could, making its way out of the wilds of Northern California into an ever-larger world.

So it ends up on a line of printers. Worse things have happened to noble missions. And if this is any consolation, the trend had just discovered yet another diasporic partner. The oldest boomer was sixty-two and now at war with aging, which meant getting serious about health, which meant getting serious about diet. Increasingly, boomers were all about it when it came to wellness eating. They could be relied upon to turn up at a barbecue and say things like, "Have you ever noticed how much sugar you drink?"

There are 93 million boomers in America. Even if only 30 percent of them underwent an "artisan redemption," this would be very good for the artisan. Plus, they are busybody know-it-alls and therefore effective diffusion agents. Indeed, by this time they were hounding their own children to feed their grandchildren better. Chances were Gens X, Y, and Z had already gotten the message. The younger you were, the more likely you were to think that eating vegan was not a fringe activity but a sensible idea. The artisan message was storming the nation. In 2011, Dana Steinberg was prepared to offer this deeply optimistic view:

> The food system in the United States is undergoing a remarkable shift. The revival of small farms and artisanal producers has generated new partnerships with restaurants, institutional food services, and retail outlets to make locally sourced, sustainably produced food more widely available. This shift has stimulated, and is now responding to, a growing demand from health-conscious consumers in ways that are affecting America's economy as well as its eating habits and well-being.[2]

But we shouldn't go too far. In 2009, there were only thirty-five hundred CSA initiatives.[3] This figure tells us that CSAs had yet to capture a significant place in the imagination of American consumers or a place of any significance in the economy. (This despite the fact that it was a very useful way of sustaining organic farms, an important staging area of the movement.) This key piece of the artisanal idea was active but not well distributed.

The artisan movement had transformed places like Brooklyn and Boulder. It had changed certain restaurants and bars. But had it touched the lives of people in the mainstream? Insisting on kale in 2008 didn't prove anything. American lives are constantly touched by the fads and fashions born in someone else's cultural galaxy. We embrace them merely to remain au courant, to "go with the flow."

Still, the artisanal revolution was conspicuous enough to draw the attention of industry. In 2010, an anonymous observer said:

> This year, big business continued to follow the foodie dollar, co-opting and transforming the language of the culinary crowd. A few years ago they swarmed the once-crunchy cottage organic industry. Then everyone from Whole Foods to Wal-Mart latched on to the "local" label. When the Big Foods of the world made Frito-Lay's Tostitos from "Artisan Recipes" and Sargento shredded cheeses from "Artisan Blends" (all trademarked, of course), you know the term lost its credibility.[4]

The artisanal movement had attracted the attention of marketers keen to get in on the trend. This is a bad place for a trend to be: merely acknowledged by consumers and now more and more fully exploited by marketers.

A couple of years later, the novelist and essayist Jen Doll took a look at the artisan trend transforming the worlds she knew in Brooklyn and upstate New York. Her first reaction was to suggest that the artisanal trend was overexposed. She wrote an obit in *The Atlantic*. It begins:

Artisanal, a word that fought early in his career to ensure recognition of craftsmen for their important contributions to society before later being drafted into the creation of a worldwide gourmet branding glut, died Wednesday.[5]

Every long-form journalist has a hunting license. All of them want to be the first to bag a new trend, the first to see it coming into or going out of fashion. There are bragging rights and book deals for those who get it right and almost no penalty for those who get it wrong. So Jen Doll may have been reaching, but as we have seen, she wasn't far off. The artisanal trend was both undersubscribed and overexposed. Life was hard. Doll's proposition: surely, it must also be short.

A year later, Jen Doll herself supplied an answer. She declared that the artisanal trend was not exhausted, not exploited, not in fact dead. Tongue still firmly in cheek, Doll was now prepared to rescind the obit she had written the year before:

> Artisanal has a radioactive half-life so powerful that it could for years sustain full-fledged underground communities of humans making bread from hand-picked cornhusks and locally sifted flour. Artisanal is not dead, it's undead, a whole food zombie running around feasting on artisanal brains. Artisanal, regardless of an organic beefsteak tomato through the heart or a hand-hewn bamboo stick to the brain, is eternal. Eternally damned, maybe, but sticking around and torturing us nonetheless.[6]

Well, this is perhaps not a complete recantation. The artisanal thing was not dead, but undead. This clever recovery hints at a larger development. By 2013, the artisanal trend had managed to install itself as an enduring part of our culture.

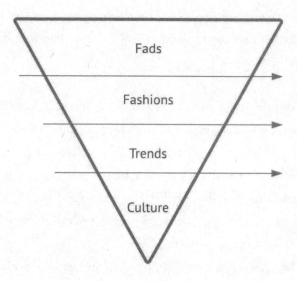

How some innovations settle into culture.

And that culture teems with change. A river runs through us. At the top, there is a flood of fads. They come whistling out of the worlds of music, design, dance, architecture, movies, TV. And most of them just keep going. They pour through. A few prove to be keepers, and they settle. Indeed, we could think of our culture as a settling tank. Most fads keep going, but a few stick around. They have weight. They capture interest. Some of these fads settle to become fashions; some of these fashions settle to become trends; some of these trends settle to become cultural realities. A year after her obit, Jenn could see that settling tank at work. The artisanal trend was increasingly a feature of our culture, here for the longer term, but not, of course, forever. (Because in our culture especially, nothing is forever.)

This was good news for several reasons. The Harvard economist Larry Katz could see the artisanal movement might be one answer to the employment crisis now upon us. He figures that "good" middle-class jobs might come from the reemergence of artisans. PBS's Paul Solman asked whether Brooklyn hipsters could help save the middle class. Ward picked up the refrain.[7] It was also true that people are beginning to question traditional career arcs, the ones that took you out of college into a city to pursue a glorious professional career.[8] For many in Gens Y and Z, it was beginning to look like these traditional careers would not be forthcoming. In an article called "The (Not So) Simple Life" a woman called Alissa Morris is quoted as saying:

> "People are starting to realize that they are detached from their food, priced out of real estate, and can't obtain any sort of American dream unless they make a major move."[9]

Here two problems, food and career, combine to inspire a move out of the city to the countryside. But of course this made sense. Who would want to suffer underemployment in the city when an artisanal life in the small town or the countryside held out the promise of new careers and styles of life?

It was no easy task liberating a diet that had been taken captive by Mad Men marketing and every "taste breakthrough" of which the food industry was capable. But the word was out. The revolution was in play. Things were beginning to change. And by the second decade of the century, the changes were marked:

> On average, American adults now eat more whole grains, nuts, and seeds, and they drink less soda. . . . But we're not eating any more fruits and vegetables than we used to, nor less salt, saturated fat, or processed meats, such as hot dogs and bologna. Plus, while Americans of various races and income levels improved their diets over

the last 15 years, richer, better-educated, white Americans improved the most, widening the gap between the country's privileged and underserved.[10]

By 2019, virtually all of the artisanal food indicators were up. Livestock and poultry products stood at $2.5 billion, up 12 percent. Vegetables at $2 billion, up 27 percent. Fruits at $2 billion, up 44 percent. Livestock and poultry at $1.6 billion, up 44 percent. Field crops $1.2 billion, up 70 percent. Some $2.04 billion in organic products were sold to retail. Another $300 million were sold directly at farmer's markets, on-farm stores and stands, roadside stands or stores, u-pick, community supported agriculture farms, and online markets. The conventional retail channel was carrying more organic products and less conventional channels were growing too. This made for fatter margins for the farmer. And by most accounts this was still critical as farms struggled to survive.[11]

So much for the organic artisanal. The growth and new stability of handmade artisanal is even more remarkable. We can use Etsy as our rough measure, and the stats there are striking. After Etsy was founded in 2005, the early days were rocky. But the second decade of the century shows tremendous growth.

The number of active buyers rises from 10 million in 2012 to 40 million in 2018. The number of sellers doubles (roughly from 1 million to 2 million). By 2019, there were 60 million products listed for sale. The percentage of sales from outside the United States now stood at 34 percent, which means artisans now had access to large international markets. And perhaps most important, 92 percent of Etsy buyers felt they couldn't find Etsy products anywhere else.[12]

Several trends were responsible for Etsy's astonishing growth, but one was perhaps key. Personalized, customized, individualized goods mattered more and more as the kind of thing people wanted to own, and they really mattered as the kind of thing people wanted to give as gifts. Artisans were the obvious beneficiary of this trend. After all, it was they who had helped create the idea and launch the reality. The movement was beginning to harvest the world it helped create.

THE COVID MOMENT

The arrival of COVID-19 in 2020 transformed the American economy and culture in many ways. It was manifestly bad for hotels, airlines, restaurants, anyone who supplied restaurants, performing arts, live music, gyms, and country fairs. It was (mostly) good for people who were selling online or could seize new opportunities there. (Etsy-based artisans were quick to bring face masks to market; at their height, masks made up a tenth of all Etsy sales.)[13] To say COVID was a mixed blessing would be an understatement.

But in one way COVID was unambiguously good news for the artisanal movement. People began to flee the city for suburbs, exurbs, small towns, and the countryside. By some estimates, three hundred thousand people left New York City, heading to upstate New York and the far end of Long Island. Sometimes this meant merely activating summer homes. Sometimes it meant renting. Sometimes it meant purchase. For all, it meant giving up their treasured city, at least for a while.

Most of these people were not migrants. They had no intention of staying. After all, a real New Yorker scorned the idea of the "bridge and tunnel" world beyond the city. This was the world God created for suburbanites, "breeders," the weak of head and heart, people without real cultural currency, those who choose to wallow in the wasteland of popular culture.

Bridge and tunnel is the world so heartlessly captured by Christopher Guest in *Waiting for Guffman*. In this "mockumentary," Guest gives us a town called Blaine, Missouri, a place were everyone is a clueless hick except for one man, Corky St. Clair. Corky is in fact a total dunce. Corky has failed to make it on Broadway and returned to Blaine to start again. Poor Corky. When he realizes that Blaine too must betray him, he lashes out.

"And I'll tell you why I can't put up with you people: because you're bastard people! That's what you are! You're just bastard people!"[14]

In a culture where expressions of outrage are crafted for us by the best writers in Hollywood, "bastard people" seems a little ineffectual. This was Guest's point exactly. In bridge and tunnel world, people aren't really very good at anything. They can't even manage convincing indignation.

The bridge and tunnel stereotype had long kept New Yorkers in place, in check, at home. Things could get very bad in the city—you could lose your job. You could fail to complete that novel or win that contract. But until you actually left the city, you were still a New Yorker, an insider. You were not yet Corky St. Clair.

The artisanal movement managed to shift this stereotype. It helped us see small towns and the countryside as a virtuous choice, instead of a Corky-scale failure. With the artisanal lens in place, the world outside of New York City became a more attractive place. Human scale, handmade, historical, authentic, kinder, gentler, less competitive. Quite suddenly, bridges and tunnels were less a source of shame than a method of escape.

But it wasn't just COVID, of course. Thanks to broadband and apps like Zoom, it was of course possible to live anywhere. And for the many New Yorkers confined to tiny apartments, the city was the last place they wanted to be. Besides which, the city was growing more violent. Over the July Fourth weekend of 2020, sixty-four people were shot and eleven killed. August was even worse. By September, financial firms and big Midtown companies were pleading with Mayor Bill de Blasio to do something.[15] Eventually, he did. He cut funding to the police.[16]

Some people began to hear echoes of the 1970s and early '80s, when the city suffered from so much unemployment and lawlessness that people began to leave, taking their taxes with them and pushing the city into a downward spiral. Fifty years later, New York City appeared poised for yet another fall. Three hundred thousand people left. Fewer people threatened a small tax base, fewer services, and more chaos. This would mean diminished police and fire support. This would mean more crime and chaos. This would mean more flight. A self-renewing cycle had been set in train.[17]

New Yorkers are perpetual motion machines. And now that New York City was pushing (thanks to COVID and crime) and places like upstate New York were pulling (thanks to the artisanal revolution), departure felt like a compelling option.[18]

What a gift for the revolution! Every small town got an infusion of people. In the early part of 2020, Litchfield, Connecticut, got two thousand newcomers in a period that would normally bring them sixty.[19] Most came bearing the big salaries that can be made in a big city. And virtually all these people had been inducted into the artisanal movement while still living in the city, by the diasporic chefs doing Waters's work there. They were newcomers, but not entirely unwitting when it came to local culture.

This is what every social movement dreams of. New recruits who are sophisticated and well-heeled. For people living in a subsistence economy, barely eking out an artisanal existence, this was water in the desert, manna from heaven. Restaurants flourished. CSAs finally passed their break-even point. Farmer's markets filled to overflowing. Life was good, or at least better.

But, of course, there is always a tension. The newcomers might grasp the general idea of the artisanal mission, but some of the realities escaped them. They could be rude and clueless. In Winhall, Vermont, the locals were feeling a bit overwhelmed:

> The post office ran out of available P.O. boxes in mid-June. Electricians and plumbers are booked until Christmas. Complaints about bears have quadrupled. And as far as the [town] dump is concerned, as [one town resident] put it, "the closest word I can tell you is sheer pandemonium."[20]

In the worst cases, the newcomers were driving real estate prices up and old-timers out. The irony was palpable. Writing from the small town of Kingston, New York, Sara B. Franklin warned of the "potential loss of people who've kept our community vibrantly diverse, not to mention alive and functioning."[21]

Still. The COVID moment brought together people with taste, money, and commitment with locals who had been making small towns and artisanal economies work for generations. Sometimes it worked; sometimes it didn't. But generally speaking, the artisanal movement was massively augmented.

The key question was whether the newcomers would stay. And this depended on a series of smaller questions. Would they put down roots? Would they "take" to life outside the big city? Would their employers let them stay, or would they call everyone back to headquarters the moment it was safe to do so?

I did a research project on American families in the COVID era.[22] Mothers were clear on whether they wanted to go back to work outside the home. For most, the answer was a resounding "no." These women now had proof that they could work from home. And now that they were working from home, they looked back at the pre-COVID era with a sense of puzzlement.

"Why was it," one of them asked me, "that we had to spend all that time commuting, all that time on our clothing and hair, all that time in the office with lots of empty engagements and pointless meetings? For what?" In the ensuing conversation, some women were prepared to entertain the suspicion that work had been a kind of "theater." This had nothing to do with functionality or practicality. My respondents thought something else was going on. One of them said:

> I think it must be men. Women can do lots of things at the same time. We can work at home. We can manage a family. It's men who need to have a separate time and place to work. They need a box to work in. It's also a question of ego. Men like to see cars in the parking lots. Why do women go into the office? They do it to satisfy male egos in the C suite.

But it was not just women who took this point of view. The *New York Times* talked to a guy who gave up his home in LA and bought a place in Vermont. Apparently, Jonny Hawton "finds it hard to conceive of returning to his old commuter lifestyle, which allowed him only an hour a day with his 1-year-old daughter."

> If someone told me I had to go back to do that tomorrow, I don't know what I would do," he said. "It's almost like we were in a trance that everyone went along with. I used to see Millie for an hour a day. This whole crisis has kind of hit the reset button for a lot of people, made them question the things they sacrificed for work.[23]

These folks will want to stay outside the city, and they are prepared to make extraordinary sacrifices to do so. The research told me that these women had used the time saved in the COVID era to change their families, to get to know their kids better, to build new relationships with their daughters, to restructure mealtime, and to give the family new centrality. At one point I thought I was looking at the possibility of the emergence of a more fully, more emphatically matrifocal family.[24]

The economist Jed Kolko is right to call for caution: "How people behave in a pandemic is probably not a great guide to how they want to live their lives in normal times. We are living in the middle of a grand forced experiment, but we really don't know how the experiment is going to play out."[25]

But there are plenty of reasons people might want to remain out of the city. For some, living in the country completes their artisanal redemption. Others were anchored in the fundamental changes in family wrought by the COVID disruption. It's worth pointing out that these changes are almost always invisible to the economist and the C-suite. This means they will be invisible to corporate America, at least for a while.

We can say this much with relative confidence: the artisanal revolution started by Alice Waters in the late '60s was brought to maturity by the COVID migration. For many artisans, there was now enough wealth and scale to promote the experiment beyond subsistence and at least suggest the possibility that the artisanal approach was now thoroughly installed in American life. More to the point, the migrants brought with them pools of talent, wealth, know-how, and network connections that could only enrich the artisanal hinterland. For the artisan who needed legal, strategic marketing, or innovation help, it was now just down the street, and possibly even free.

ARTISANS AFTER COVID

Much of what we do, and who we are, will be changed by COVID. As Kolko says, it is hard to know what awaits us. But what I want to do in this section is discuss one tempting scenario: that artisans could be our future.

Of course, caution is called for. It's very possible that the new normal will look very like the old normal. We will go back to work. Cities will return to form. It will take a Studio 54–level blowout to get the COVID period out of our system, but then we will get over it. It will take months, perhaps years, to restore our economy, but this, too, will happen. Even our institutions of higher education will return to something like normal.

I grant this possibility, but I want to at least entertain an alternative future. This one says change is coming, from an artisanal direction. Consider the following scenario. (I offer it not as a perfect prediction, but so that we prepare ourselves for a situation that, should it arrive, will be less painful and more manageable for our opportunity to think it through.)[26]

RECRUITING MILLENNIALS

Millennials and Gen Z (hereafter "millennials" for short) have on the whole been refused a berth on the industrial economy. This was a trend long before COVID, but it has been greatly accelerated. We will see millennials acting as both a cause and an effect of our artisanal future.

Millennials made extraordinary efforts to get into college. Some of them set aside completely the "youth culture" available to (some in) previous generations. They came out of their undergraduate experience burdened by enormous debt. They competed once more for places in graduate schools, law schools, and business schools, amassing even more debt, only to discover that these did not guarantee them jobs. The digital revolution was shrinking the accounting, financial, and legal professions. Houses were expensive. Children were expensive. This generation felt the effects of the 9/11 attacks and then a succession of recessions, one of them so bad it was called the Great Recession. All this misfortune piled up. The *Washington Post* wondered if millennials might be "the unluckiest generation in U.S. history."[27]

Then came COVID. The *Wall Street Journal* put the bad news in a headline: "Millennials Slammed by Second Financial Crisis Fall Even Further Behind":

> The economic fallout of the Covid pandemic has been harder on millennials, who are already indebted and a step behind on the career ladder from the last financial crisis. This second pummeling could keep them from accruing the wealth of older generations.[28]

Who wanted a conventional career path when it now looked like pushing a boulder up a very high hill? How tempting to find a craft or a creative process that might set you free. The artisan does this beautifully. All of the definitions we noted in chapter 5 can be read as an opportunity to walk away from the middle-class existence. I am not suggesting that the artisan movement was crafted for this purpose, just that it can work this way.

HELP FROM A DECENTRALIZING AMERICA

American cities were already losing their allure before COVID. Sabrina Tavernise and Sarah Mervosh found that New York, Los Angeles, and Chicago had all lost population over the last few years. Even before COVID, millennials were choosing places like Tucson, Raleigh, and Columbus, as well as exurbs and newer suburbs outside large cities.[29] With COVID, New Yorkers were particularly keen to get out of the city in what *Forbes* called "droves."[30]

In the end, COVID would injure all parts of the American experiment, but it would affect the city first and foremost:

> Now, as local leaders contemplate how to reopen, the future of life in America's biggest, most dense cities is unclear. Mayors are already warning of precipitous drops in tax revenue from joblessness. Public

spaces like parks and buses, the central arteries of urban life, have become danger zones. And with vast numbers of professionals now working remotely, some may reconsider whether they need to live in the middle of a big city after all.[31]

The exodus was being driven by two much larger trends: the career crisis experienced by young people and the deteriorating state of the cities themselves.

HELP FROM A DECLINE OF CONSUMPTION

But this was just for starters. There were other trends at work. We can see the decline of traditional standards of consumption. I see this in my ethnographic interviews. People tell me that conspicuous consumption is too, well, conspicuous and therefore to be avoided. Showing off, once that great American pastime, is now frowned upon. Or to use a new phrase, if you must brag, do it humbly.[32]

This comes through especially in the new trend known as "normcore." The term was created by a trend-forecasting collective called K-HOLE. Fiona Duncan describes normcore fashion as

"ardently ordinary clothes. Mall clothes. Blank clothes. The kind of dad-brand non-style you might have once associated with Jerry Seinfeld, but transposed onto a Cooper Union student with William Gibson glasses."[33]

This was a wild act of repudiation. So much of American culture and the American economy had centered on declaring one's specialness. To dress in a manner "ardently ordinary" really was to tip things over. Fashion was about claiming some membership, some difference, and the possession of wealth, taste, and discernment. To wear ordinary clothing was simply to step out of American culture. It was also to withhold your dollars from the American economy. But most of all, it signaled a willingness to take your leave of the usual patterns of sociality. What took you away from these drew you closer to the artisanal, if indeed it did not deposit you there.

HELP FROM A DECLINE OF COOL

Perhaps still more radically, we have witnessed, in recent years, the decline of cool. Cool was a withholding of enthusiasm. It was the enemy of sincerity. It was especially keen to distance itself from the mainstream and middle class, anything earnest, eager, or conformist. Cool was the particular possession of youth and a way to scorn creatures of age. Cool kept its distance.

And then quietly, over the last couple of decades, cool began to cease to matter. If it pleases the court, let the record show two quite different social creatures, both of them prepared to betray cool.

Let's start with Chance the Rapper, an artist at the heart of surely the coolest part of contemporary culture, hip-hop. There may not be anyone cooler than Chance the Rapper. I'm just saying. This guy is massively talented, famous, and loved. And what did he do at the height of his greatness? He wrote a love song to his grandmother. Rock and roll does not normally acknowledge the elderly. In fact, I am certain that the words "grandma" and "grandpa" do not appear anywhere in the hip-hop lexicon or anywhere else, for that matter, in the history of rock and roll.

In a song called "Sunday Candy," Chance the Rapper writes:

> . . . your grandma ain't my grandma,
> mine's handmade, pan-fried, sun-dried . . .[34]

In "Familiar," Chance the Rapper heaps scorn upon women who are trying for cool, the ones who turn up in the latest fashion. The key lyric is "forgive me but you look familiar," and Chance turns the pickup

line into criticism. Women grasping for cool are excoriated for their efforts. (Language alert: some of what follows will offend some readers as
misogynistic.)

> She the latest model but these hoes retros
> One in a million, but these bitches special . . .
> But you just so usual, you just look used . . .[35]

Cool is scorned. Grandmothers are cherished. Fashionistas are predictable.

Chance the Rapper criticizes his own pursuit of cool. In "Wanna Be
Cool," the lyric runs:

> All the confidence I was tryin' to buy myself
> If you don't like me, fuck it, I'll be by myself[36]

And it's not just there. We also see the disavowal of cool in the pages
of the *Times Literary Supplement* (TLS) and on its accompanying podcast.
Until recently, the editor of both was a man called Stig Abell.

You don't have to listen to this guy for very long to understand that
he is a prodigious talent, that he has read the entire canon, and that he
can field virtually any literary topic with gusto and ease. He is, in short,
just the kind of guy you would expect to occupy this position. He is a
particularly fine token of a distinguished British type.

But the next thing you notice about Abell is that he is no creature of
orthodoxy. He openly admits to reading books that are scorned by virtually everybody with literary pretensions. Abell says he reads Lee Child's
Jack Reacher books and, gasp, that he likes them.[37]

This is really wild. Cheeky even. Most serious people don't usually
read Jack Reacher novels, and if they do they often have the decency
to register embarrassment and regret. Most criticism, of any art form,

engages in this kind of virtue signaling, meant to show how deeply considered and fine is the critic's sensibility. After all, membership in the tribe always matters more than the task at hand.

Apparently, Abell can manage without this public performance of the self. He even reads historical fiction, much of which is middlebrow stuff and, well, just not done. (I know you understand this, right? You and I, we're good?) What we get from Abell, in place of fineness, is boldness. This is not boldness of the competitive kind, the one that stakes a claim to more than its share of a conversation. It's boldness in aid of clarity, as an act of emphasis.[38] (Or put it this way: this is not bold as in personality, but bold as in typeface.) Abell spends no time on identity signaling. Every author, genre, topic, and title is on the table. Curiosity is all, and the starter's gun has sounded.

What we see in Chance the Rapper and Stig Abell is a repudiation of cool. They do not care that their enthusiasms define them as enthusiasts. They don't care to signal distance. They are untroubled by the possibility that we might think them suckers for middlebrow fiction or the worship of elders. These guys are earnest in earnest. This makes them perfect fellow travelers for the artisanal movement.

The best symptom of the decline of cool may be the state of cool hunters, a community that once helped organizations find their way in a confusing, chaotic culture. The trouble is that the sky is falling. Where once there were tens of trends, now there are hundreds of them. This is too many for one person, even a sensationally hip person, to keep track of. Now cool hunters can be found running around on airport runways dodging jumbo jetliners with the rest of us.

The three Cs—cities, consumption, and cool—used to keep people out of the artisanal world. It just seemed so folky and clueless. Surely, red-check flannel could only take you so far in the world. Surely, all that manual labor obscured the real opportunity of a contemporary culture, the digital revolution that opened creativity to millions of people. Surely, when so many of us now have the training, the inspiration, and the permission to make our own culture, the artisanal version of DIY, all hammers and tool belts, just seems a little too literal.

Yet, as I will argue in the next chapter, artisans retain a Promethean aura. It does feel like they are doing something extraordinary for contemporary culture. If creativity is now for everyone, the artisans are the ones fashioning a place for this creativity to take up residence. And especially as people stream out of the industrial economy and the big cities, artisans are the ones welcoming them across.

The future has gotten faster, meaner, and less intuitive. And it's not like we weren't warned. Joseph A. Schumpeter told us that capitalism inclined naturally toward creative destruction. Alvin Toffler diagnosed our "future shock." Peter Schwartz pitied organizations trapped in a state of "perpetual surprise." Clayton Christensen warned of "disruption" of an essential feature of the contemporary world. Nassim Nicholas Taleb told us we must fear "black swans," changes that so departed from our expectations we could not imagine them. We were warned.[39]

Taleb is right. There is something out there coming, even for the artisan. It's hard to imagine, because they are the darlings of the moment. We're the ones who invented the world, so of course, we perfectly match the world. But this, too, shall pass. The world will move on. The danger here is smugness, which has proven the downfall of every fashion trend, political party, and mighty corporation. Smugness is the beginning of the end.

What is our black swan? It will be a shift in sensibility, a new worldview, a new aesthetic. And it may already have arrived. It might be sitting right under our noses. And we can't see it, because again we define the moment. Anything that doesn't look like us must be wrong or, in Taleb's point of view, invisible.

Ask the celebrity starlet, athlete, or talk show host, the one who just rose to prominence. They are exalted because they don't just reflect the moment; they define it. But their celebrity must eventually slip away. It will happen by gradual stages. A fickle public will move on. New stars will emerge. These will look like pretenders and the existing stars will dismiss them. But the public will not, and one or two will flourish.

This fall must eventually happen to the artisan. More and more people will cease to care about the artisanal approach. Eventually, even the loyalists drift away. We will end up standing in the parking lot of the Beverly Hilton during the Golden Globe Awards, hoping for an interview. Someone like the TV show *TMZ* will indulge us, if only to ridicule us: "Hey, Harvey, you'll never guess who showed up at the Golden Globes!" And everyone will have a good laugh at our expense.

Is there a contender out there now? Almost certainly. My wife and I went to a restaurant in London called Pollen Street Social. It was my birthday. My wife is a foodie. She chose. The meal was a revelation for me. It was like a tabletop laboratory. Our meal came to the table throwing flames and belching smoke. A tiny, controlled disaster. (What better way to celebrate the birthday of an aging anthropologist?) More important, it was miles away from the usual pieties of the artisanal restaurant.

Is this it? Will we be supplanted by the molecular gastronomy movement? Could this be what Chez Panisse was in 1971? Probably not. But this is proof that some black swans are assembling, a change that entirely contradicts our point of view.

It's hard to see the other challengers, but we can easily see the takedown artists. Virtually the whole of Portlandia, for starters. And Brooklyn has come in for its share of scorn.[40] The artisanal feeling for the exquisitely careful choice in coffee and beer is now a target.[41] Cultural trends, at the top of their game, present themselves as inevitable. The comics are now giving us a chance to see that the artisan is arbitrary.

So the future is coming, and it won't have a place for us unless we prepare. Certainly, we should emphasize our strengths. Take, for instance, our gift for making the world homey and cozy. This is one of the ways we show we are anti-industrial. It's what happens when we commit to the imperfect and the handmade. Cozy has certain values wired into its very scale. It's hard to treat someone badly when you know you are going to see them again tomorrow at the diner. Finally, cozy is also an excellent way to welcome migrants from the mainstream. It signals that we are a place of sharing and caring, that we exist for the relationship, not the transaction; for the community, not the competition.

But cozy has a danger. It can make us provincial, un-cosmopolitan, narrow, and self-congratulatory. At its base, the artisanal has a world-renouncing impulse, a refusal of what's happening "out there." Many of us come to the artisan community not just to avoid alternatives, but to repudiate them.[42]

And in some ways, this is fair. Every social movement works to make members feel like a group, to make them feel what Goffman called a "we."[43] But it's a bad thing if it yanks us out of the stream of contemporary life. Recall the hippies in chapter 2 stopping the commune truck by driving it into a tree. Repudiation mustn't become self-sequestering. We must trade with the world, if only to keep our antibodies up.

Social media is built for this task. YouTube is the raw feed of contemporary culture. It's an observation platform from which we can engage in a range of social experiments. So is Facebook. For all its relentless missteps, it also helps us see all the new species of social life taking shape in the world, and to build an audience for our own galaxy. And once we have a connection, Twitter helps us stay in touch with friends and fans telegraphically. Instagram is the stage on which we perform, the place we show our latest wares. And when we see the work of someone else in the artisanal community, someone who wows us with their imagination and creativity, social media makes it easy to reach out and make contact. Social media wires us into the world out there and enables to recruit those who might join us.

But there is a second way to preserve a place in the world. And that's to keep ourselves and our communities porous. We want to emphasize the moral clarity that is our signature, of course we do, but we don't want to harden our boundaries. The inclination for some artisans is to construct an identity that is monolithic and well armored. This may feel like the path to authenticity, but it is also a surefire way to lock ourselves into a fixed adaptation.

What we want is selfhood and a community that's porous. This lets things in. It's almost respiratory. Things come in. Things go out. Freed from single-mindedness and fixity, we can flow with alternatives. We are mobile.

"Multiple selves" turns out to be one of the secrets here. This is a somewhat grand term for the sensation that we are more than one person. The best illustration of this is that thing that happens when you are having lunch with someone who thinks you are one person and are joined at the table by someone who knows you as another person. Awkward!

Or take the case of Stewart Brand, as I discussed in chapter 3. Brand was a great accumulation of selves sourced from his Stanford learning, Army training, Merry Prankster bus rides, rooftop visions, the things he published, the organizations he organized.

Multiple selves are very useful to the artisan. You may actually experience several different artisan selves as you find yourself responding to different parts of the world. There may also be future artisan selves that you glimpse from time to time, when you see something interesting and think, *Hmmm, I wonder what it would be like to do X?*

And then there are the things I am going to talk about now, all the acts of creativity and innovation and world building that it takes to keep our galaxies alive. These also serve to pull us out of ourselves, to cultivate new points of view. Here a well-stocked portfolio of selves gives us a distinct adaptive advantage.[44]

Here's where I make an argument that might seem anti-artisanal. I want to argue that for all of our historical continuity and groundedness, we are obliged to stay current with all the things that are happening in and around our culture.

Fashion, even fashion. It's easy to scorn fashion. Isn't this, we ask, one of the symptoms of a consumer society and convincing proof that this is a world that cannot separate what is serious from what is frivolous? Well, that is the fashionable thing to say about fashion. Indeed, in the senior(s) common room at our great universities, it is the necessary thing to say. But some people see a deeper significance to fashion. The great French geographer Fernand Braudel (1902-1985) thought fashion might actually be essential to the Western gift for self-transformation. He asked,

> Can it have been merely by coincidence that the future was to be-
> long to the societies fickle enough to care about changing the co-
> lours, materials and shapes of costume, as well as the social order and
> the map of the world societies, that is, which were ready to break
> with their traditions? There is a connection.[45]

The notion here is that we can see in the colors, materials, and shapes of the fashion world a glimpse of the worlds that are in the works. And this I would argue is essential for those who would pilot an artisan community. As I note above, we are the darlings of fashion at the moment, but this will not last forever.

We want to monitor the world. There is a steady stream of innovation taking place everywhere, the world of social media, gaming, storytelling, design thinking. You name it and someone is tinkering with it.

Now that the future comes at us like a gale from the North Sea, prior acquaintance is a very good thing. It's easy to be complacent. It's easy to imagine ourselves as deep and thoughtful creatures with weightier concerns than passing fashions. But we need to be listening more carefully than ever. Imagine yourself a mezzo-soprano, humming while washing dishes at the sink. This is likely the least interesting sound you will make this week, but that doesn't mean it's not an opportunity for illumination. Every so often something will surface. A stray refrain will activate your gift. "Oh, what's that?" you ask as a particularly fetching melody sambas by. "How interesting." Entire worlds have come from less.

7

THE FUTURE

A NEW ARTISANAL COMMUNITY

We can see the future of the artisan. What we don't see we can build. That's what we're going to do now. Detect and devise. Fish out your red pencil and correct me as we go.

When I think of the future of the artisan, I think of the flourishing of communities outside the bigger cities, almost a parallel civilization. By 2030, these are substantial. Some people have come to call them the "Labs." We don't know why. But for some reason it sticks. ("Cantons" was in the running for a while. Then it died. "What?" someone asked. "You want us to sound like Switzerland?")

The starter kit for this parallel world was all the stuff we've talked about so far, the sixty years that from the advent of the counterculture to the early twenty-first century. The steady repudiation of the industrial era, the rise of a new approach to craft, farming, food, restaurants, and markets, the advent of new patterns of sociality and community, the emergence of leaders like Alice Waters and Stewart Brand. The industrial economy was scaled down, made more local and, ironically, less and less industrial. A "walk to town" trend was bringing people into closer contact. Cities were being made to feel more like small towns. This parallel world was human scale and handmade. It was a world built by, and for, artisans.

By the start of the twenty-first century, everyone had heard of the artisan. Most people actually knew several by name. And there were lots of fellow travelers, people who were cultivating a beehive, a community garden plot, or a handcraft of their own. A shockingly large number of Americans were prepared to call themselves foodies. Farmer's markets, health food stores, and craft fairs were now mainstream.

This was not what we could call a triumph. The artisanal option was visible, but well off its full ascendancy. It remained an add-on to American culture, interesting but still marginal. The artisanal movement was caught in what mariners call slack water, the moment between the rising and falling tide when the water just sits.

Then came COVID. By March 2020, American culture was grinding to a standstill. Schools and workplaces emptied out. Millions went home and stayed home. And within days, Americans, the lucky ones, began to stream out of the cities. They moved into small towns and the countryside. They were able to leave thanks to new technologies like Zoom, but the fact that there was someplace they wanted to go, that was all culture. That was the work of the artisans. The artisans had built a community outside the cities. A starter kit. A platform. The beginnings of an ecosystem. And now that there were new people with more money, it could grow.

The newcomers were water in the desert. Artisans had a larger audience. Many restaurants could sense a lifting tide. Farmers were feeling less marginal. Craftspeople had a sudden increase in "coreligionists" fresh from Michaels and Hobby Lobby. This meant new, more practiced patrons. People were feeling a little more flush. Adjustments had to be made, and some artisans simply couldn't adapt. But for some people, the COVID era was a time to rise out of subsistence into something a little more secure.

Skeptics insisted this was a fleeting prosperity. "Don't get used to it," they warned. "People have been fleeing plague cities for centuries. And for centuries they have returned the moment it was safe to do so. COVID plenty was fool's gold, and artisans who thought otherwise were kidding themselves."

And sure enough, as vaccines rolled out and herd immunity grew nearer, you could see a return to the cities. Actually, a lot of people went back to the city and partied like it was 1999. People went a little nuts. "See," said the skeptics, "the COVID bounce is over. The cities are back in business. And you are out of luck." Things looked grim for the artisans. They had lost their stroke of good fortune.

Not so fast! After people got the Studio 54 moment out of their systems, they began to think again. Maybe they didn't want to live in the city after all. They looked around them. What they saw was sad, dangerous, chaotic, and struggling. And some of them thought, *Hmmm, this isn't what I remember. And this isn't what I want. Not for my family. And especially not for my kids.* You could almost feel cities seizing up like ancient, exhausted mechanical engines.

There would be no simple restoration of the city after all. The whirlpools of crime and confusion would not let up. The city struggled mightily, but it could not escape its entropy. Life remained tippy and chaotic. Corporations tried calling people back to headquarters and an astonishing number said no. Urban economies faltered, public life shriveled, crime grew, and still more people left. The cities had stalled.

It turned out that the COVID "bounce" was a keeper. The small towns were getting richer. They were actually growing. And as cities pushed people out, the towns were pulling them in. Migrants came from everywhere. As 2020 unfolded, they came in such numbers it wasn't clear where to put them. The towns were now flying like Jules Verne airships. City dwellers looked up in wonder.

You could see why the towns were doing so well.

The artisan economy was deeply embedded in a social and cultural world. This was a gestural economics. A little jar of jam suddenly turns up on your doorstep. Personal relationships flowed with generosity, as you woke up to discover someone clearing your driveway after a snowstorm. Your clothing was created by a friend. And that was weird. Passing the person in town who made your sweater and seeing them look with interest at the patches you added to the elbows. The café you went to for your morning coffee was also the place your daughter did spoken word on Thursday night. The Little League diamond was where people gathered to greet the sun and start the day.

Commercial transactions were set in a relationship, as if by a jeweler. The hardware store owner was also the volunteer ambulance driver. The librarian was teaching little kids how to read, teenagers how to talk about what they read, and parents how to write that novel they'd been planning for so long. In fact, the entire enterprise of education seemed to blossom. Everyone in town who knew anything was prepared to share it with others.

And everyone seemed to get better at teaching, better at the visualizations and a new TED-scale brevity. People took new pride in how local kids were flourishing intellectually. Inevitably, someone would look around at this community buzzing with knowledge and say, *You know, we could actually create a college.* (To which someone would reply, "Who says we're not?") And now that real colleges were collapsing intellectually and financially, this seemed like an increasingly urgent thing to do.

Business savvy, the toughest part for many artisans, was flowing freely. (So many of the newcomers came to town bearing new capabilities.) In fact, some towns were beginning to act like brilliant business incubators. Venture capital and angel investors started showing up. And someone had to take them aside and say, *There's a very good chance you don't know how this place works, that business is community and that community is business. But listen, stick around, and maybe you'll get the hang of things.*

For would-be migrants, the overall effect was dazzling. Who wouldn't want to live in this cauldron of creativity and initiative? More humane, more interesting, and you could make a living.

One of the things that defined these unnaturally alert communities was their loathing for "externalities." As in, they didn't want any. Externalities are the things that capitalism produces when it pollutes the air and water. In these newly prosperous towns, externalities were not allowed. And this meant people spent a long time thinking about recycling, sustainability, and producing clean water and air. They got quite good at it. And this added a layer of knowledge to the small-town consciousness.

To help with this effort, people decided to recruit engineers who could create the technologies necessary for carbon offsetting, hyperloops, and biofuel. They learned how to contend with microplastics, nuclear waste, chemical solvents, and other persistent pollutants. These men and women didn't always look or act like artisans, but they were embraced as essential colleagues. And most of them mastered the artisanal approach in no time.

The Labs were buzzing with so many enterprises, these artisans discovered that one of the things they had to learn to make was consensus. At first everyone just looked at one another, as if to say, *How in god's name are we going to do what so few Americans seem capable of doing?* In the end, this turned out to be a skill like any artisanal skill. You got better at it, the more you did it. You built it, you fixed it, eventually you perfected it.

And some people achieved "master craftsperson" status. The best of them were so good, Labs competed to bring them in. The best solution: to rotate these people from Lab to Lab, with issues set aside for their return. This was just one of the ways that the Labs were now serving as a laboratory for the rest of American culture, in this case cultivating a gift for conflict resolution that seemed to escape non–Lab Americans.

People kept asking, "So, are you guys a commune?" And the answer was "partly 'yes,' but mostly 'no.'" There are things we share (dome) and things we don't (grid). The dome, on the one hand, is the place we give freely. We don't keep track. We ask people to give for the openhanded pleasure of giving. You gave to the dome for intrinsic reasons, not to get something in return. Grid, on the other hand, that is, consists of everyone's small patch in the world, where they make their decisions and take responsibility for what happens there. This duality of dome and grid maximizes generosity and minimizes conflict.

So crafted, the Labs didn't just grow; they evolved. They became more complex. They got better at doing the things they knew they needed, better even at things they never dreamed they could do. Artisans, it turns out, could do many things. They could even build worlds.

The Labs built worlds so well, solving so many problems of contemporary life, that lots of people wanted to live there, and they began to come in droves. Relatively speaking, the Labs were still only 15 percent of the US population. But people kept saying they were "where the energy was." The Labs were flourishing while the rest of the American experiment felt like it was running out of gas.[1]

Actually, the rest of the American experiment no longer looked like an experiment at all. Especially the big, ugly, noisy, broken cities. These were haunted by crime and unemployment. They were the captives of vested interests and old orthodoxies that didn't care they didn't work. This became a standing joke at meetings in the Labs. If you needed an easy laugh, something to break the tension at a meeting, all you had to do was throw in the name of a big-city mayor. Everyone would laugh out loud and move on. "De Blasio" got the best laughs.

Then an interesting thing happened. The Labs grew out of their physical boundaries. Their generosity began in the near world, family, friends, neighbors. Lab-ness began to travel outwards, to embrace perfect strangers. The Lab's empathy circle was expanding. The Labs stood ready to help even those who were not really much like Lab dwellers at all.

Some Labs were not defined by space or region at all. You could join some Labs (the "virtual" ones) and continue to live in Florida, Iowa, or Mexico. The Labs started as something geopolitical. Now it was launched as something thoroughly cultural and entirely mobile. It could go anywhere, and it did. This was a helpful corrective for those Labs that tended to act too much like a small town, refusing difference and departure. When the Lab moved into the world and the world poured in, both places were somehow oxygenated.

The Labs were even helping recraft the social architecture.

By the beginning of the twenty-first century, many of the traditional differentiators in American society were beginning to look a little outdated. Did a degree from a great university really make a big difference in someone's life? Not really. Did a high-powered job? Probably not. Did wealth? Did race? Did gender? Perhaps not. Social differences in the twentieth century might as well have been tattoos. Now they felt a little less permanent, more negotiable, and, in many cases, less special.

The Labs helped make it clear how easy it was to live without these differences, the tattooed ones. First, people questioned the differences. Then they ceased to believe in them altogether. Well, of course, there were "Porsche holdouts" from the 1 percent. These were the people who continued to protest their difference, their specialness. But where once they might have been admired, now Lab citizens were more likely to look at one another and murmur, "Who is he trying to convince? Protesting too much, much?"

If there was a hierarchy in the Labs, it favored people who knew how to do things. Honor belonged to the best artisans. But this standing did not accumulate. The fact that you were really good at raising goats, fashioning consensuses, or being an eco-engineer got you some admiration, and nothing more than that. It didn't mean you had access to more wealth, power, or standing. You were just admired for being good at that one thing. There was a reputation economy, but it did not confer big houses or Porsches on anyone.[2]

So people with social standing took a hit. The Lab had built a world that did not need or revere them. They got back into their Porsches and roared out of town. Hey, where they were going, McMansions were plentiful and cheap! Nor did the Labs need corporations like General Motors, General Electric, or General Mills. This was not a world of brand messages. It was a world of personal meanings. Certainly, there was still a place for big corporations, but increasingly they serve the American economy in new ways.

Still, there was a problem. Artisans, being all about the tradition and continuities of their craft, are inclined to prefer a world that stays the same. As we have noted, this is a chronic problem and a serious one. The Labs could not afford to lose touch with the furious invention taking place in the world at large.

Something had to be done. The old artisanal dog had to be taught new tricks. So, by general consensus, an allowance was made to include crafts that had been previously discouraged or neglected. One of these was the design of indie sneakers. Sneakers are artisanal in some ways. For the indie producer, shoes are handmade in small batches. The trouble is that almost everything about shoes is an abomination from an environmental point of view, requiring materials and solvents that are terrible for the environment.[3]

Still, the good thing about sneakers is that they are deeply embedded in the world of street fashion that had effectively taken over the world of conventional fashion. If you could just solve the environmental problem, this was an opportunity. To have someone who could compete in this industry would give the Labs a very useful window on contemporary culture. The Labs reached out to Annie Mohaupt, the brilliant Chicago artisan who makes shoes for the more traditional fashion industry and who just happens to be all about the sustainability issue. Hey, presto. A solution to the problem, plus the presence of someone else who could help keep the Labs more fully "in the mix."[4]

Another way to open the world is to embrace the world of small film production. The great thing about this world is how tidal it is. Films are made by communities of people who come to a town, stay for two to four months, and then leave. The Lab gets infusions of capital without the permanent installation of a company that may or may not share Lab values.

I did a little digging and discovered that the Hudson Valley Film Commission has managed to welcome five hundred film productions since 2000. This has brought in $250 million in regional development to Dutchess, Orange, and Ulster counties in New York State.[5]

This is a princely sum, but it also represents the infusion of creative people who can be relied upon to share some of their sophistication, even if they come and go a bit more than the true locals.

A third possibility is a laboratory that creates synthetic creatures, aka synths. These are creatures that simulate a human being. The first generation are merely CGIs (computer-generated images). But even these are evolving rapidly, and some now serve as fashion models, including creatures like Shudu Gram and Miquela Sousa. The Canadian model Sinead Bovell looks on:

Miquela Sousa is a 19-year-old Brazilian American model, influencer, and now musician, who has amassed a loyal following of more than 2 million people on Instagram. She's collaborated with Prada and Givenchy, has been featured in a Calvin Klein video with Bella Hadid, and she just released a song with singer-songwriter Teyana Taylor this past spring. Impressive stuff, but there's one thing that's keeping real-life me at ease: Miquela . . . is a computer-generated image (CGI).[6]

As these creatures evolve, they will be equipped with AI (artificial intelligence) and then released into the world. They will start by living online. We will interact with them in game space and on various forums. We will come away from some conversations wondering, *Wow, was that a real person or a synth?* But they can also be dropped into the "real world," thanks to Augmented Reality software. Eventually, they will be equipped with a physical presence. The endgame here is not a facsimile of a human. We are looking for verisimilitude. As Bovell notes, "their creators aren't just designing them as avatars, but also giving them entire backstories, personalities, and causes to champion." What an extraordinary craft this would be. Imagine a Lab that creates synths. It would require (and develop) deep cultural knowledge and deep technical knowledge. A good Lab wants both.

We have found a way to make a river run through us. In the case of sneakers, we get to see what is happening at the bleeding edge of fashion innovation. In the case of synths, we can participate in the bleeding edge of digital innovation. In the case of filmmaking, we can watch and listen as people craft content for a still broader audience. All of this is good for us.

One Lab will surely specialize in mapping the future. As the world gets more turbulent, every organization needs navigational advice. In some versions of this profession, there is grand talk of AI, robots, big data, immense databases. That's not my experience. For many purposes, reading the future will require an artisanal approach, with data being pooled, curated, and analyzed piece by piece and each insight assembled, buffed, and polished by hand. Here, too, we end up with something we can sell to the world that has the added benefit of producing a stream of intelligence we can use for ourselves. Call me if your Lab needs a map.[7]

Labs will need to find the middle course. Some of our truths are incontrovertible: human scale, handmade, raw, local, historical, and un-branded. We oppose "externalities." We are careful of the planet. We are committed to sustainability. These are our fundaments.

But some of what and who we are will have to change as the world does. We can't expect to just slide into the future. We are going to have to build and rebuild ourselves as we go. This should be possible. After all, we are good at crafting things. Why not a world of constant renovation, by ourselves, for ourselves?

But I get it. Asking artisans to build the artisanal world, that's tough. We already have a job. Hands are full. Minds preoccupied. Asking an ar-tisan to invent the future is like asking an artist to build an art museum in which her work will hang. Committee meetings? Fundraising? Ex-hibit design? "No. No. No. You don't get it," says the artist. "I'm a dream catcher. Things come whistling, murmuring, shimmying into my head, and it's my job to get them into the world. I can't be going to committee meetings!"

Too bad. If we want to survive, we will have to learn to change con-stantly. More important, if we want to make ourselves a real alternative to the mainstream, we will have to change constantly. No, it wouldn't be easy. But check out our roster. We have an anthropologist prepared to act as an artisan. And artisans prepared to act as anthropologists. What could possibly go wrong?

The future of the artisan could look like this. Thousands of commu-nities of artisans spread across the country. When I see them in my mind's eye, they look the way towns do when you see them from an airplane at night. A small cluster of orange glowing in a black landscape, suspended there like a galaxy in the heavens.

These tiny communities, with the help of millions of Americans, had managed to take on and defeat the dietary-industrial-cultural system that stood astride the twentieth century organizing identity, aspiration, and standing, telling us what we wanted, who we thought they were, and where we stood in the world.

The artisanal revolution helped demolish conspicuous consumption. It punctured luxury. It has ridiculed the symbol systems signaling distinctions and standing. Yes, of course, we still make distinctions, we still use money and symbols to "front," as the kids used to say. But this is now a rear-guard action, a kind of theater in which we are all actors, unconvincing and unconvinced, at the end of a very long run. Not much enthusiasm, precious little conviction, mostly *Mousetrap* exhaustion.[8]

Taking down the industrial-dietary-cultural complex took sixty years and the efforts of an Alice Waters and Stuart Brand, millions of hippies and foodies, all those farmer's markets and craft fairs, and people saying no to a vast and reckless diet of sugar, fat, salt, nicotine, and alcohol. We managed to beat back fast food, prepared food, and sometimes even breakfast cereal. It took thousands of crafty people who manage to bring new imagination and creativity to the world of goods.

Was it hard? It was pretty hard. Was it the artisan's biggest challenge? Not really. That starts now. Taking down the industrial-dietary-cultural complex was the warm-up. But now we must take on a more formidable enemy. Our task in the future is to take on the future.

APPENDIX

"Uncle Meyer's Wallet"
Toronto Globe and Mail, August 21, 1990

U ncle Meyer died in his sleep on August 4. He was 82 and lived
with his wife in a north Toronto high-rise. He worked as a volunteer at an animal shelter. He went for long walks. He was a truly
sweet guy, but not a very candid one. He didn't wear his heart on his
sleeve. He didn't regale you with the "Uncle Meyer" story.

Except once. One night after dinner, Uncle Meyer brought out his
photographs. I froze. This is the relative's great fear: caught without de-
fenses when the photographs come out.

Uncle Meyer did it perfectly. He just materialized at the dinner table,
photos in hand. I felt myself struggling for an excuse. Weren't we double-
parked in a fire zone on a traffic island? Didn't the sitter need a drive
home to Rochester? Uncle Meyer had us. We bowed to the hard dictates
of good form.

And there it was. Lying under the photographs was a wine-colored
canvas wallet, about the size of a paperback. It was stitched together boldly,
and in places crudely with thick green thread. "What's this?" I asked, already in the object's thrall. Uncle Meyer looked up at me and then back
at the wallet. "Oh, that," he said and stopped.

I picked it up, anthropologist on alert. The wallet was what we might call, after Proust, a "Madeleine" object: an object charged with meaning and power.

Madeleine objects have lots of powers. Sometimes they cut away the present time and place, and transport us—in Proust's case to the embrace of a childhood bed and maternal attentions. But sometimes they have a different character altogether. Sometimes they come at us airborne and night-flying.

Uncle Meyer's wallet was one of these. It reached up and gave me a crack across the snout. The last time I'd seen anything like this, I'd been peering into a museum display case, a Yale University art historian beside me. We have been doing what academics tend to do, parading manners and theories.

We stopped to comment airily on something, and an Inuit mask came up out of the case like a shark from water. The voracious energy of the thing. Hah! We were suddenly little men in suits blinking stupidly. Uncle Meyer's wallet opened a cut on the surface of reality. Something dangerous came spilling into life.

And tactile. So tactile. Somehow it managed to be both personal and completely traditional. You could see that it conformed to a traditional pattern to which generations had contributed. But it was also the work of an individual in the throes of a terrible emotion driving the stitches in one direction and then another. There was craft here and there was something craft couldn't contain.

Uncle Meyer was slow to tell the story, but eventually he did. The wallet was stitched 65 years ago by his mother. She made it to hold his passport and the Canadian visa that would see him safely out of a land of terror, pogroms, and state-sanctioned anti-Semitism.

Meyer was then 17. He could leave Russia. His family could not. His father died of natural causes, he told me. "My mother, well, the Nazis . . . I don't know what happened."

Meyer arrived in Canada in 1925, going first to Montreal and then to Edmonton to work for a relative. He spent the early years moving back and forth across the country, a member of a team of Jewish roughnecks who worked on the construction of big buildings from Victoria to Kingston.

There was, after all, nothing dreary or domestic about Uncle Meyer's photographs. They were taken from the dizzying heights of construction sites: the Banff Springs Hotel, the Vancouver Medical–Dental Building, grain elevators across the prairies. Meyer painted those elevators. He and his pals liked to ride the wooden platforms as they banged around in high winds.

Meyer's canvas wallet brought him to another country and another life. He lived, despite his roughneck heroics, safe from harm. He escaped the holocaust that claimed his family.

He had come away from his home and his family with a few clothes and not much more. As his mother prepared him for his departure, as she prepared herself for the fact that she would likely never see him again, she took up thread and canvas. She made a wallet for his passport, so that her reckless, bounding son would not lose the paper that would see him into safety. She produced an envelope to see Meyer into the envelope of the new world. Meyer made it. The wallet worked.

ACKNOWLEDGMENTS

This book was a long time in the making and thanks are especially due to my wife, Pamela DeCesare, for her many contributions, intellectual, empirical, and spiritual. Thank you, sweetie!

This book is a product of the Artisanal Economies Project. Special thanks are due to co-founder Sam Ford, who in his thoughtful, intelligent, strategic way found solutions that were beyond me. The project and this book would have been impossible without him.

Thanks are due to its board members, patrons, supporters, and participants: Thomas Ball, Jennifer Bayles, Emily Carleton, Kevin Clark, Theresa DiMasi, Bob Eydt, Gerry Flahive, Craig Frazier, Katarina Graffman, Jodi Harris, Mary Hogarth, Leora Kornfeld, Eric Kuhn Drew Lamm, Guy Lanoue, Samantha Lubash, Mark Miller, Scott Miller, Bill O'Connor, Bill and Harriet O'Neil, Chris Perry, Ivy Ross, Marissa Shrum, Ken Skovron, Stephanie Smith, Peter Spear, Jack Stahl, Wendy Stahura, Lisa Werenko, Bob and Marilyn Wiles-Kettenmann, Sara Winge, and Bert Xanadu.

I am grateful to the following people for more general, but not less valuable, contributions: David Alworth, David Armour, Dorie Bledsoe, Bud Caddell, Rob Campbell, Kristen Cavallo, Pip Coburn, Edward Cotton, Lauren Culbertson, John Curran, Mark Earls, Camper English, Rob Fields, Allyson Forstrom, Scott Gilmore, Nick Gillispie, Eric Glasgow, Michele Goodman, Ric Grefé, Tom Guarriello, Kate Hammer, Jodie Harris, Charles Heller, JC Herz, Lauren Hoken, Barbara Holzapfel, Sam Hornsby,

ACKNOWLEDGMENTS

Larry Katz, Mateo Kehler, Steve King, Tara Koger, Joan Kron, Eric Kuhn, Peter Laywine, Anne Lewison, Ed Liebow, Max Luthy, Sofi Madison, Diana Magna, Leland Maschmeyer, Emmett McCusker, Betsy and David Mettler, Robert Morais, Eric Nehrlich, Indy Neogy, Jerry Nevins, Lauren Parker, Gregory Parsons, Gwen and Joan Peterdi, Lizzie Shupak, Drew Smith, Ruth Soenius, Patti Sunderman, Cheryl Swanson, Sophie Wade.

NOTES

INTRODUCTION

1. Steve King, Anthony Townsend, and Carolyn Ocklels, "The New Artisan Economy," Institute for the Future, 2008, http://http-download.intuit.com /http.intuit/CMO/intuit/futureofsmallbusiness/SR-1037C_intuit_future _sm_bus.pdf.
2. To test this assertion, I searched the terms "artisan" and "artisanal" in Amazon to a depth of one hundred entries.
3. Scott Pelley, "AMEX CEO Touts 'Small Business Saturday,'" CBS News, November 21, 2011, accessed October 9, 2014, http://www.cbsnews.com /news/amex-ceo-touts-small-business-saturday/.
4. Jason Mick, "Wendy's New 'Natural Fries' Caught Using Chemical Stew," DailyTech, April 16, 2011, http://www.dailytech.com/Wendys+New+Natu ral+Fries+Caught+Using+Chemical+Stew/article21394.htm.
5. "Since 2000, the U.S. has seen 5.8 million manufacturing jobs shift overseas.
6. Nick Reding, *Methland* (New York: Bloomsbury USA, 2009), Kindle location 106): "The economy and culture of Oelwein [Iowa] are more securely tied to a drug [i.e., methamphetamine] than to either of the two industries that have forever sustained the town: farming and small business."

CHAPTER 1
THE BEGINNING: INDUSTRIAL AMERICA

1. John Kenneth Galbraith, *The Affluent Society* (Boston: Houghton Mifflin, 1958): "The family which takes its mauve and cerise, air-conditioned, power-

steered and power-braked automobile out for a tour passes through cities that are badly paved, made hideous by litter, blighted buildings, billboards and posts for wires that should long since have been put underground. They pass on into a countryside that had been rendered largely invisible by commercial art . . . They picnic on exquisitely packaged food from a portable icebox by a polluted stream and go on to spend the night at a park which is a menace to public health and morals. Just before dozing off on an air mattress, beneath a nylon tent, amid the stench of decaying refuse, they may reflect vaguely on the curious unevenness of their blessings. Is this, indeed, the American genius?" (p. 223). Newton Minow, "Television and the Public Interest: An Address to the National Association of Broadcasters, Washington, D.C.," 1961, American Rhetoric, accessed September 27, 2010, http://www.americanrhetoric.com /speeches/newtonminow. htm.

2. Edwin C. Breeden et al., *The American Yawp*, edited by Joseph Locke and Ben Wright, 2 vols. (Stanford, CA: Stanford University Press, 2018), http://www .americanyawp.com/text/26-the-affluent-society/#identifier_5_117.

3. Robert A. Nisbet, *Social Change and History: Aspects of the Western Theory of Development* (New York: Oxford University Press, 1969).

4. Matt Novak, "Push-Button Promises," *Pacific Standard*, January 25, 2013, updated June 14, 2017, accessed September 27, 2020, https://psmag.com /environment/push-button-culture-51858.

5. Alfred P. Sloan, *My Years with General Motors* (Garden City, NY: Doubleday, 1963), p. 323.

6. Herbert Brean, "'54 Car: 3 Years Old at Birth," *Life* 36 (3): 80–92; Penny Sparke, *A Century of Design: Design Pioneers of the 20th Century* (London: Mitchell Beazley, 1998); Bevis Hillier, *The Style of the Century, 1900–1980* (New York: Dutton, 1980), p. 146; Frances Basham, Bob Ughett, and Paul Rambali, *Car Culture* (New York: Plexus, 1984).

7. Grant David McCracken, "When Cars Could Fly: Raymond Loewy, John Kenneth Galbraith, and the 1954 Buick," in *Culture and Consumption II: Markets, Meaning, and Brand Management* (Bloomington: Indiana University Press), pp. 53–90.

8. For an excerpt of the performance in which Seinfeld talks about Pop-Tarts: https://youtu.be/YmCTUBEluSE.

CHAPTER 2
THE AWAKENING: HIPPIES AND THE COUNTERCULTURE

1. Donald R. Katz, *Home Fires: An Intimate Portrait of One Middle-Class Family in Postwar America* (New York: HarperCollins, 1992); Elaine Woo, "Susan Lydon, 61; Author of Influential Feminist Essay," *Los Angeles Times*, July 25, 2005, https://www.latimes.com/archives/la-xpm-2005-jul-25-me-lydon25-story.html.

2. Jonathan Kauffman, *Hippie Food: How Back-to-the-Landers, Longhairs, and Revolutionaries Changed the Way We Eat* (New York: William Morrow Paperbacks, 2019), pp. 2, 5.

3. Todd Gitlin, *The Sixties: Years of Hope, Days of Rage* (New York: Bantam Books, 1987), p. 209.

4. Stewart Brand, "Summer of Love: 40 Years Later," *SFGate*, May 20, 2007, https://www.sfgate.com/news/article/Summer-of-Love-40-Years-Later-Stewart-Brand-2559651.php.

5. Joe Samberg in Jennie Rothenberg Gritz, "The Death of the Hippies," *The Atlantic*, July 8, 2015, https://www.theatlantic.com/entertainment/archive/2015/07/the-death-of-the-hippies/397739/.

6. Erika Anderson, "What Life Is Like When You're Born on a Commune," *Vanity Fair*, August 2014, accessed September 3, 2020, https://www.vanityfair.com/news/daily-news/2014/08/the-farm-born-on-a-commune.

7. "Father Yod," Wikipedia, last modified May 24, 2021, 22:16, https://en.wikipedia.org/wiki/Father_Yod.

8. Jonathan Kauffman, *Hippie Food* (New York: William Morrow, 2018, Kindle), p. 7.

9. Jon Wiener, "When Abbie Hoffman Threw Money at the New York Stock Exchange," August 24, 2017, https://www.thenation.com/article/archive-it-was-50-years-ago-today-abbie-hoffman-threw-money-at-the-new-york-stock-exchange/.

10. Dominic Hood, "Harvard Explained," *Harvard Crimson*, October 2002, https://www.thecrimson.com/article/2002/10/24/harvard-explained-where-does-the-phrase/.

11. Grant McCracken, *Chief Culture Officer: How to Create a Living, Breathing Corporation* (New York: Basic Books, 2009), pp. 74–76, http://www.amazon

.com/Chief-Culture-Officer-Breathing-Corporation/dp/0465018327, pp. 74–76.

12. Josh Karp, *A Futile and Stupid Gesture: How Doug Kenney and National Lampoon Changed Comedy Forever* (Chicago: Chicago Review Press, 2006); Legs McNeil and Gillian McCain, *Please Kill Me: The Uncensored Oral History of Punk* (New York: Grove Press, 2006).

CHAPTER 3

THE PIONEERS: ALICE WATERS, STEWART BRAND, AND MARK FRAUENFELDER

1. Tom Wolfe, *The Electric Kool-Aid Acid Test* (New York: Picador, 2008), p. 2.
2. Fred Turner, *From Counterculture to Cyberculture: Stewart Brand, the Whole Earth Network, and the Rise of Digital Utopianism* (Chicago: University of Chicago Press, 2006), p. 62.
3. Stewart Brand, "Summer of Love: 40 Years Later," *SFGate*, May 20, 2007, https://www.sfgate.com/news/article/Summer-of-Love-40-Years-Later-Stewart-Brand-2559651.php; Adam Hirschfelder, "The Trips Festival Explained," Experiments in Environment: The Halprin Workshops, 1966–1971, January 14, 2016, https://experiments.californiahistoricalsociety.org/what-was-the-trips-festival/.
4. Turner, *From Counterculture to Cyberculture*.
5. Stewart Brand in Walter Isaacson, *The Innovators: How a Group of Hackers, Geniuses, and Geeks Created the Digital Revolution* (New York: Simon & Schuster, 2014), p. 271.
6. Anna Wiener, "The Complicated Legacy of Stewart Brand's 'Whole Earth Catalog,'" *New Yorker*, n.d., accessed October 22, 2020, https://www.newyorker.com/news/letter-from-silicon-valley/the-complicated-legacy-of-stewart-brands-whole-earth-catalog.
7. Isaacson, *The Innovators*, p. 20.
8. Wiener, "The Complicated Legacy of Stewart Brand's 'Whole Earth Catalog.'"
9. Turner, *From Counterculture to Cyberculture*, p. 135.
10. David Brooks, "Opinion: The Man Who Changed the World, Twice," *New York Times*, May 7, 2018, https://www.nytimes.com/2018/05/07/opinion/stewart-brand-hippie-silicon.html.
11. Wiener, "The Complicated Legacy of Stewart Brand's 'Whole Earth Catalog.'"

12. Mark Frauenfelder, *Made by Hand: Searching for Meaning in a Throwaway World* (New York: Penguin, Kindle, 2010).

13. Ibid., p. 50.

14. Anonymous, "DIY Simplest Automatic Pet Feeder with Arduino," Maker Pro, June 26, 2019, https://maker.pro/arduino/projects-diy-simplest-automatic-pet-feeder-with-arduino.

15. Rebecca Kesby, "Technology: How the World's First Webcam Made a Coffee Pot Famous," BBC News, November 22, 2012, https://www.bbc.com/news/technology-20439301.

16. Clifford Geertz, *The Interpretation of Cultures: Selected Essays* (New York: Basic Books, 1973).

17. Anonymous, "Rube Goldberg," n.d., http://en.wikipedia.org/wiki/Rube_Goldberg.

18. This image of Rube is clipped from an image created for the *Literary Digest* and published there on April 12, 1919. The image consists of self-portraits supplied by fifty-two editorial cartoonists. Wikipedia says this image exists in the public domain. https://commons.wikimedia.org/wiki/Category:Rube_Goldberg#/media/File:Editorial_cartoonists'_self-portraits_(1919).png.

19. Grant McCracken, *Culturematic: How Reality TV, John Cheever, a Pie Lab, Julia Child, Fantasy Football . . . Will Help You Create and Execute Brilliant Ideas* (Boston: Harvard Business Review Press, 2012), p. 38.

20. Cliff Kuang, "Eye Candy: OK Go's Insane Rube Goldberg Machine," *Fast Company*, March 2, 2010, accessed July 6, 2010, http://www.fastcompany.com/1567383/eye-candy-ok-gos-insane-rube-goldberg-machine.

21. E. Mazareanu, "FedEx Express: Total Average Daily Packages 2020," Statista, July 2020, https://www.statista.com/statistics/878354/fedex-express-total-average-daily-packages/.

22. Jordan Vallejo in Brendan O'Connor, "A Simple Task: Inside the Whimsical but Surprisingly Dark World of Rube Goldberg Machines," The Verge, April 22, 2015, https://www.theverge.com/2015/4/22/8381963/rube-goldberg-machine-contest-history-ideas.

23. Thomas McNamee, *Alice Waters and Chez Panisse: The Romantic, Impractical, Often Eccentric, Ultimately Brilliant Making of a Food Revolution* (New York: Penguin, 2007), Kindle locations 1582–83.

24. Ibid., Kindle locations 253–57.

25. Marian Burros, "Home & Garden: What Alice Taught Them: Disciples of Chez Panisse," *New York Times*, September 26, 1984, https://www.nytimes.com/1984/09/26/garden/what-alice-taught-them-disciples-of-chez-panisse.html. I can't find the original article in *Gourmet* magazine, which has gone out of business. But the article is referenced here on Fodor's website: https://www.fodors.com/community/united-states-best-restaurants-usa-gourmet-magazine-01-a-205744/.

26. Paul Freeman, "How Food Became Chic," *Yale Alumni Magazine*, September/October 2017, accessed October 26, 2020, https://yalealumnimagazine.com/articles/4575-how-food-became-chic.

CHAPTER 4

TEN WAVES AND THREE TOWNS:
A MOVEMENT GROWS, FROM CONNECTICUT TO KENTUCKY

1. Several women have accused Mario Batali "of sexual harassment . . . [and he] has been charged with indecent assault and battery stemming from an allegation that he groped and kissed a woman at a Boston restaurant in 2017." As of May 23, 2019, he has denied the charge. "Mario Batali Charged With Assault and Battery in 2017 Case," *New York Times*, May 23, 2019, https://www.nytimes.com/2019/05/23/us/mario-batali-charged-boston.html.

2. This list is a partial list. It excludes precedents like Helen Evans Brown, *West Coast Cook Book* (New York: Little, Brown, 1952), and alternate views, for which see Todd Kliman, "How Michael Pollan, Alice Waters, and Slow Food Theorists Got It All Wrong: A Conversation with Food Historian and Contrarian Rachel Lauden," *Washingtonian*, May 29, 2015, https://www.washington.com/2015/05/29/rachel-lauden-how-michael-pollan-alice-waters-got-everything-wrong/. For a historical overview, see Joyce Goldstein and Dore Brown, *Inside the California Food Revolution: Thirty Years That Changed Our Culinary Consciousness* (Berkeley: University of California Press, 2013).

3. Paul Freeman, "How Food Became Chic," *Yale Alumni Magazine*, September/October 2017, accessed October 26, 2020, https://yalealumnimagazine.com/articles/4575-how-food-became-chic.

4. Oliver Schwaner-Albright, "Food: Brooklyn's New Culinary Movement," *New York Times*, February 24, 2009, https://www.nytimes.com/2009/02/25/dining/25brooklyn.html.

5. Ronda Kaysen, "Food Start-Ups Flock to Old Pfizer Factory in Brooklyn," *New York Times*, March 27, 2012, http://www.nytimes.com/2012/03/28/business/food-start-ups-flock-to-old-pfizer-factory-in-brooklyn.html.

6. Benjamin Wallace, "The Twee Party: Is Artisanal Brooklyn a Step Forward for Food or a Sign of the Apocalypse?", *New York*, April 13, 2012, http://nymag.com/news/features/artisanal-brooklyn-2012-4/.

7. David Black, "The Sixth Borough," [Hudson, NY] *City Journal*, July 14, 2017, https://www.city-journal.org/html/sixth-borough-15334.html.

8. Grant McCracken, "Frank Capra Capitalism?", Medium, March 12, 2018, https://medium.com/@grant27/frank-capra-capitalism-c2ffc94a524e. See the video in this post for more on Lenihan's vision.

9. Ann Barr and Paul Levy, *The Official Foodie Handbook: Be Modern—Worship Food* (New York: Arbor House, 1985).

10. Ben Schaffer, "The Local: How Dale DeGroff's Epochal Blackbird Revitalized Cocktail Culture," *Rum Reader*, July 2020, https://www.rumreader.com/the-local-how-dale-degroffs-epochal-blackbird-revitalized-cocktail-culture/.

11. Camper English, "Has the Mixology Movement Created a Monster?", 7X7SF, February 2011, http://www.7x7.com/eat-drink/has-mixology-movement-created-monster.

12. Tom Acitelli, *The Audacity of Hops: The History of America's Craft Beer Revolution* (Chicago: Chicago Review Press, 2013).

13. Jordan Weissmann, "Americans Now Drink More Craft Beer than Budweiser," *Slate*, November 24, 2014, http://www.slate.com/blogs/moneybox/2014.11/24/budweiser-sales-decline-americans-now-drink-more-craft-beer-than-bud.html?wpsrc=fol_tw; E. J. Schultz, "Young Drinkers Have Abandoned Big Beer—Can It Be Saved?", *AdAge*, October 1, 2014, http://adage.com/article/cmo-strategy/beer-industry-debates-mainstream-beers-fixed/295222/.

14. Tim Carman, "Why Fast-Casual Restaurants Became the Decade's Most Important Food Trend," *Washington Post*, December 31, 2019, https://www.washingtonpost.com/news/voraciously/wp/2019/12/31/why-fast-casual-restaurants-became-the-decades-most-important-food-trend/.

NOTES

15. Andrea Blázquez, "Whole Foods Market Statistics & Facts," Statista, n.d., https://www.statista.com/topics/2261/whole-foods-market/.

16. Zoya Gervis, "Here's How Many Americans Consider Themselves 'Foodies,'" *New York Post*, May 28, 2019, https://nypost.com/2019/05/28/heres-how-many-americans-consider-themselves-foodies/.

17. Anonymous, "2019 Organic Survey Results Show Sales Up 31% from 2016," news release, United States Department of Agriculture, October 2020, https://www.nass.usda.gov/Newsroom/2020/10-22-2020.php.

18. Isabel Angell, "Annie's CEO Defends General Mills Buyout of Organic Food Company," KQED, September 2014, https://www.kqed.org/news/147250/annies-ceo-defends-general-mills-buyout-of-organic-food-company.

19. Alicia Wallace, "Natural Grocery Stores Are at Risk as Organic Goes Mainstream," CNN Business. February 2020, https://www.cnn.com/2020/02/25/business/organic-mainstream-natural-foods-grocers-survive/index.html.

20. Raphael Brion, "Watch Lewis Black Slam the 'Artisanal' Food Trend," Eater, May 2, 2012, https://www.eater.com/2012/5/2/6590799/watch-lewis-black-slam-the-artisanal-food-trend; Josh Ozersky, "The 'Artisan' Hoax: Has That Word Become Meaningless?", *Time*, May 2, 2012, https://ideas.time.com/2012/05/02/the-artisan-hoax-has-that-word-become-meaningless/; Benjamin Wallace, "The Twee Party," nymag.com, April 13, 2012, accessed October 22, 2014, http://nymag.com/news/features/artisanal-brooklyn-2012-4/.

21. Anonymous, "Artisanal Capitalism: The Art and Craft of Business," *The Economist*, January 4, 2014, https://www.economist.com/business/2014/01/04/the-art-and-craft-of-business.

22. Duncan LaBarre, "32 Etsy Statistics You Need to Know in 2020," *Veeqo* (blog), September 10, 2020, https://www.weeqo.com/us/blog/etsy-statistics.

23. I want to take this opportunity to thank Monty Sommers for encouraging me to think like this.

24. "Darien Connecticut," Wikipedia, last modified May 24, 2021, 21:16, https://en.wikipedia.org/wiki/Darien,_Connecticut.

25. I have written about Ken before: Grant McCracken, *The New Honor Code* (New York: Simon & Schuster, 2021), pp. 38–43.

26. Ken Skovron in ibid., pp. 41–42.

27. This is surmise on my part. I reached out to Ms. Waters. She declined an interview.

28. Erving Goffman, *The Presentation of Self in Everyday Life* (Harmondsworth: Penguin, 1959).

29. Anonymous. "Roton Point," Rowayton Historical Society, n.d., https://www.rowaytonhistoricalsociety.org/roton-point.

30. Frank Raymond, *Rowayton on the Half Shell: The History of a Connecticut Coastal Village* (West Kennebunk, ME: Phoenix, 1990), p. 101.

31. Deborah Wing Ray and Gloria P. Stewart, *Norwalk: Being an Historical Account of That Connecticut Town* (Canaan, NH: published for Norwalk Historical Society by Phoenix Publishing, 1979), p. 161.

32. Lisa Prevost, "Real Estate: Where Norwalk and Darien Collide," *New York Times*, January 14, 2014, https://www.nytimes.com/2014/01/19/realestate/where-norwalk-and-darien-collide.html.

33. Cliff Coady, "New York: The View From Rowayton; a Yacht Club Survives Condos and Pretensions," *New York Times*, May 23, 1993, https://www.nytimes.com/1993/05/23/nyregion/the-view-from-rowayton-a-yacht-club-survives-condos-and-pretensions.html .

34. See figure 29 in Anonymous, Darien CDP, Connecticut Housing Data, TownCharts,n.d.,https://www.towncharts.com/Connecticut/Housing/Darien-CDP-CT-Housing-data.html. (Note that the data for Rowayton is in fact the data for Norwalk, the larger town of which it is a part. Rowayton homes might be a little larger than five rooms.)

35. Faiza Elmastry, "New US Trend: Living in a Walkable City," Voice of America, December 2015, https://www.voanews.com/usa/new-us-trend-living-walkable-city.

36. Madeline Stone, "The American McMansion Is Dying for Good," Business Insider, August 25, 2016, https://www.businessinsider.com/the-mcmansion-is-dying-2016-8?international=true&r=US&IR=T.

37. I must note that the flight from New York City created by COVID meant that Darien was once more a highly desirable place to live.

38. David Brooks, *Bobos in Paradise: The New Upper Class and How They Got There* (New York: Simon & Schuster, 2001).

39. Jane Jacobs, *The Death and Life of Great American Cities* (New York: Random House, 1961); Brooks, *Bobos in Paradise*.

40. McCracken, *The New Honor Code*, p. 36.

41. Greg Lukianoff and Jonathan Haidt, *The Coddling of the American Mind: How Good Intentions and Bad Ideas Are Setting Up a Generation for Failure* (New York: Penguin, 2018).

42. McCracken, *The New Honor Code*, p. 36.

43. The prime mover of Erin's approach to child-rearing is Lenore Skenazy, *Free-Range Kids: Giving Our Children the Freedom We Had without Going Nuts with Worry* (San Francisco: Jossey-Bass, 2009).

44. I am sorry to say that I am unable to identify the source of this story. I read it fifty years ago.

45. Grant McCracken, *Transformations: Identity Construction in Contemporary Culture* (Bloomington: Indiana University Press, 2008), http://www.amazon.com/Transformations-Identity-Construction-Contemporary-Culture/dp/0253219574/.

46. Thomas Massie in *Off the Grid with Thomas Massie,* directed by Matt Battaglia, produced by Matt and Kerry Kibbe (Washington, DC: Free the People Productions, 2018), circa 1:20. For more on this documentary, see Logan Albright, "Individualism, Independence, and Incongruity in Rural Kentucky," Free the People, October 12, 2018, https://freethepeople.org/individualism-independence-and-incongruity-in-rural-kentucky/.

47. Sam Ford and Grant McCracken, "Project Entry # 7: The True Service of a 'Convenience Store,'" *The Artisanal Economies Project* (blog), May 18, 2017, https://artisanaleconomiesproject.org/2017/05/18/project-entry-7-the-true-service-of-a-convenience-store/.

48. "Maritimers" is a term for Canadians from New Brunswick, Nova Scotia, Prince Edward Island, and sometimes Newfoundland. They are widely admired for their ability to talk. This link from Storytellers of Canada will give you a glimpse: https://www.storytellers-conteurs.ca/en/events-calendar/maritimes.html.

49. This photo taken by Grant McCracken February 23, 2019. I do not yet have Erinn's permission to use it.

50. I interviewed Erinn in Hartford, Kentucky, on February 23, 2019.

51. Erinn Williams, "The Preacher's Daughter: The Unknown," *Times-Tribune,* July 29, 2020, https://www.thetimestribune.com/opinion/columns/the-preachers-daughter-the-unknown/article_61d46f90-ee5e-5448-930c-58d60b01d341.html. See her reply to J. D. Vance's *Hillbilly Elegy* here: Erinn Williams, "The Preacher's Daughter: The Appalachia I Know," *Times-Tribune,* December 2, 2020, https://www.thetimestribune.com/opinion/columns/the-preachers-daughter-the-appalachia-i-know/article_ed8a3be4-592a-54a4-aba4-e308219b4013.html.

52. Robyn Minor, "Home Cafe & Marketplace's Ambitious Opening," [Bowling Green] *Daily News*, July 20, 2011, https://www.bgdailynews.com/community/home-cafe-marketplace-s-ambitious-opening/article_f48e0baa-5641-58ba-bda8-a6d175f89cd.html.

53. Anonymous, Kentucky Diabetes Face Sheet, https://chfs.ky.gov/agencies/dph/dpqi/cdpb/dpcp/diabetesfactsheet.pdf.

54. From an interview Sam Ford and I did with Josh Poling in a speeding car driven by Josh and going about 75 miles an hour on the way out of Bowling Green on the afternoon of March 8, 2017.

55. Picture shows Nathan Howell of Need More Acres. Taken February 23, 2019. Photographer: Grant McCracken.

56. See the very interesting video at the bottom of the page at needmoreacres.com.

57. This interview with Gavin Mann (left) and David Moore (middle) conducted at the farmer's market in Bowling Green, February 23, 2019..

58. Grant McCracken and Sam Ford, "Project Entry #2: The Peacefield Farms Interview," *The Artisanal Economies Project* (blog), April 29, 2017, https://artisanaleconomiesproject.org/2017/04/29/the-artisanal-economies-project-entry-2-the-peacefield-farms-interview/. For more on Peacefield https://peacefieldky.wixsite.com/peacefield/.

59. Marshall Sahlins, *Stone Age Economics* (Piscataway, NJ: Aldine Transaction, 1972).

60. Laurel Wilson, "Top Crops: Volunteers construct garden beds for program that assists special needs adults," *The Daily News*, August 23, 2013, https://www.bgdailynews.com/news/top-crops/article_0b3da88c-81a5-59a7-a075-fc2feed9ee3e.html.

61. Grant McCracken and Sam Ford. "Project Entry #6: When Your Business Model Is a Moral Model," *The Artisanal Economies Project* (blog), May 15, 2017, https://artisaleconomiesproject.org/2017/05/15/project-entry-6-when-your-busines-model-is-a-moral-model/.

62. Thomas H. Davenport, *Thinking for a Living: How to Get Better Performances and Results from Knowledge Workers* (Boston: Harvard Business Review Press, 2005); Thomas H. Davenport and Laurence Prusak, *What's the Big Idea?: Creating and Capitalizing on the Best New Management Thinking* (Boston, Harvard Business School Press, 2003); Richard Florida, *The Rise of the Creative*

Class: And How It's Transforming Work, Leisure, Community and Everyday Life (New York: Basic Books, 2003); Paul H. Ray and Sherry Ruth Anderson, *The Cultural Creatives: How 50 Million People Are Changing the World* (New York: Three Rivers Press, 2001); Thomas A. Stewart, *Intellectual Capital: The New Wealth of Organizations* (New York: Crown Business, 1998); Thomas A. Stewart, *The Wealth of Knowledge: Intellectual Capital and the Twenty-First-Century Organization* (New York: Doubleday Business, 2001).

63. Mark Frauenfelder, *Made by Hand: Searching for Meaning in a Throwaway World* (New York: Portfolio, 2010).

64. David Kamp, *The United States of Arugula: How We Became a Gourmet Nation* (New York: Broadway, 2006).

65. This photo (Community Farmer's Market Truck) taken by Grant McCracken, Bowling Green, Kentucky.

66. Grant McCracken, "The Coming Point-of-Sale Revolution," *Harvard Business Review*, May 6, 2011, accessed September 13, 2014, http://blogs.hbr .org/2011/05/i-gotta-hit-ya-the-coming-revo/.

67. Rachel Botsman and Roo Rogers, *What's Mine Is Yours: The Rise of Collaborative Consumption* (New York: HarperCollins, 2010); Lisa Gansky, *The Mesh: Why the Future of Business Is Sharing* (New York: Portfolio, 2010).

68. Mark Granovetter and Richard Swedberg, *The Sociology of Economic Life* (Boulder, CO: Westview Press, 1991); Sahlins, *Stone Age Economics*.

CHAPTER 5

THE RULES: TWENTY-FOUR THINGS THAT DEFINE THE ARTISAN

1. Mark Frauenfelder, *Made by Hand: Searching for Meaning in a Throwaway World* (New York: Penguin, Kindle, 2010), p. 57, emphasis in the original Derek Guyer of Kentucky Reclaimed says, "We really believe something can be perfectly imperfect, in Grant McCracken, "Product Imperfect," *The Artisanal Economies Project* (blog), May 2, 2017, https://artisanaleconomiesproject.org/2017/05/02 /project-entry-4-product-imperfection/.

2. Marc Henshall, "Vinyl's Imperfections Improve the Listening Experience," Your Sound Matters, October 2, 2017, https://www.yoursoundmatters.com /vinyls-imperfections-improve-listening-experience/.

3. Grant McCracken, "Low Fidelity Culture," CultureBy, June 16, 2010, http:// cultureby.com/2010/06/low-fidelity-culture.html.

4. The photo of P&G headquarters is from Wikipedia Creative Commons Attribution 2.0 Generic license. Photo shot by Derek Jensen (Tysto), August 9, 2005, https://commons.wikimedia.org/wiki/File:Cincinnati-procter-and-gamble-headquarters.jpg. I am told that any resemblance to the Daleks in *Doctor Who* is entirely coincidental.

5. Tom Eblen, "Millersburg Woman Turned Fried Apple Pies into a Delicious Retirement Business," *Lexington Herald-Leader*, October 4, 2015, https://www.kentucky.com/news/business/article42632499.html.

6. Kate Bernot, "Case Study: The Ale Apothecary," Beer Brewing: Brewing Industry Guide, March 31, https://brewingindustryguide.com/case-study-the-ale-apothecary/.

7. Homa Dashtaki in Nikita Richardson, "The Accidental, Surprising, Thriving Artisanal Incubator," *Fast Company*, July 16, 2015 https://www.fastcompany.com/3048309/the-accidental-surprising-thriving-artisanal-incubator.

8. David Morey and Scott Miller, *The Underdog Advantage: Using the Power of Insurgent Strategy to Put Your Business on Top* (New York: McGraw Hill, 2004).

9. Personal communication. I talked to Mr. King by phone December 16, 2020, emergentresearch.com.

10. Lexi Krock, "Stone Age Toolkit," PBS, n.d., https://www.pbs.org/wgbh/nova/clovis/tool-nf.html.

11. Peter Laslett, *The World We Have Lost*, 3rd ed. (Milton Park, Oxfordshire: Taylor & Francis, 1999). The term "satanic mills" comes from William Blake's *Milton: A Poem in Two Books*, https://en.wikipedia.org/wiki/And_did_those_feet_in_ancient_time.

12. Thomas A. Stewart, *Intellectual Capital: The New Wealth of Organizations* (New York: Crown Business, 1998); Thomas H. Davenport and John C. Beck, *The Attention Economy: Understanding the New Currency of Business* (Boston: Harvard Business Review Press, 2002); Richard Florida, *The Rise of the Creative Class: And How It's Transforming Work, Leisure, Community and Everyday Life* (New York: Basic Books, 2003); Susan Crawford, "The Origin and Development of a Concept: The Information Society," *Bulletin of the Medical Library Association* 71 (4): 380–85; Tyler Cowen, *The Age of the Infovore: Succeeding in the Information Economy* (New York: Plume, 2010).

13. Matthew B. Crawford, *Shop Class as Soulcraft: An Inquiry into the Value of Work*, reprint ed. (New York: Penguin, 2010).

14. Mihaly Csikszentmihalyi, *Flow: The Psychology of Optimal Experience* (New York: Harper & Row, 1990).

15. Please see the appendix.

16. Gary Dinges, "Lawsuit: Tito's Vodka Isn't Actually 'Handmade,'" Statesman, October 16, 2016, https://www.statesman.com/business/20161006/lawsuit -titos-vodka-isnt-actually-handmade.

17. Anonymous, "Hollow Balinese Pyramid Salt Harvested by Hand," Sun Gods Superfoods, n.d., https://sungodssuperfoods.com.au/product/balinese-sea-salt.

18. Faythe Levine and Cortney Heimerl, eds., *Handmade Nation: The Rise of DIY, Art, Craft, and Design* (New York: Princeton Architectural Press, 2008); Faythe Levine (director) and Cortney Heimerl (producer), *Handmade Nation* (Milwaukee: Milwaukee DIY, 2009). See also *Handcrafted America*, a documentary series hosted by Jill Wagner, with many illuminating interviews that take us right into the artisan experience.

19. Sue Daly, "Timber!," in Levine and Heimerl, eds., Handmade Nation, p. 74.

20. Faythe Levine, "Preface," In Levine and Heimerl, eds., *Handmade Nation*, p. xi.

21. I interviewed Tyler in 2009 as part of a research project commissioned by a client who wanted to know what the great chefs were thinking.

22. Alice Waters in Thomas McNamee, *Alice Waters and Chez Panisse: The Romantic, Impractical Often Eccentric, Ultimately Brilliant Making of a Food Revolution* (New York: Penguin, Kindle, 2007), Kindle locations 1568–69.

23. Tom Acitelli, *The Audacity of Hops: The History of America's Craft Beer Revolution* (Chicago: Chicago Review Press, 2013, Kindle), p. 24.

24. Duane D. Stanford, "Craft Beers Account for About 8 Per Cent of the U.S. Market by Volume; That Share Is Expected to More than Double by 2020, according to the Brewers Association," Bloomberg Businessweek, September 22–28, 2014, p. 29; Jan Conway, "Total Number of Breweries in the United States 2012–2019," Statista, June 24, 2020, https://www.statista .com/statistics/224157/total-number-of-breweries-in-the-united-states -since-1990/.

25. This is my phrasing of Sofi's argument. It comes from a conversation I had with her in late April 2017. Grant McCracken, "Artisanal Economies, Entry #1, The Sofi Interview, The Artisanal Economies Project (blog), https:// artisanaleconomies project.org/2017/04/29/the-artisanal-economies-entry -1-the-sofi-interview/ (blog). Here is Sofi on Instagram: https://www .instagram.com/p/CGP0TbmHFxi/.

26. Lowell L. Bryan and Michele Zanini, "Strategy in an Era of Global Giants. Sidebar: Where Complexity Hurts," *McKinsey Quarterly*, November 1, 2005, http://www.mckinsey.com/insights/strategy/strategy_in_an_era_of_global _giants#sidebar1.

27. Nassim Nicholas Taleb, *The Black Swan: The Impact of the Highly Improbable*, 2nd ed. (New York: Random House Trade Paperbacks, 2010).

28. https://en.wikipedia.org/wiki/Automat.

29. Michelle Ott, "Who Are You?" n.d., https://thepostcardmachine.com/pages /about. If you like Ott's work, you can support her on Patreon here: https:// www.patreon.com/thepostcardmachine.

30. See my effort to fix capitalism: Grant McCracken, *Culturematic: How Reality TV, John Cheever, a Pie Lab, Julia Child, Fantasy Football . . . Will Help You Create and Execute Breakthrough Ideas* (Boston: Harvard Business Review Press, 2012).

31. Evan Andrews, "Who Invented Beer?", History.com, January 8, 2014, updated September 7, 2018, https://www.history.com/news/who-invented-beer.

32. Winifred Gallagher, *New: Understanding Our Need for Novelty and Change* (New York: Penguin, 2012).

33. Jocelyn gave me permission to use this quote by email on November 17, 2020. Anonymous, "PetitFelts—Handcrafted Felted Sculptures from the Hudson Valley," The Hudson Valley Sojourner, n.d., https://www .hudsonvalleysojourner.com/crafts/other-crafts/petitfelts-handcrafted -felted-sculptures/, accessed November 18, 2020. Photo: Glenda the Fox by Jocelyn Gayle Krodman, https://www.petitfelts.com/shop/glenda-the-fox.

34. Sam Ford, "Project Entry #14: Lacey, Media Wonder Dog, and the Hustle of an Artisanal Portfolio Business," The Artisanal Economies Project (blog), August 6, 2017, https://artisanaleconomiesproject.org/2017/08/06/lacey -social-media-wonder-dog/.

35. Bren Smith, "Don't Let Your Children Grow Up to Be Farmers," *New York Times*, August 9, 2014, http://www.nytimes.com/2014/08/10/opinion /sunday/dont-let-your-children-grow-up-to-be-farmers.html. See the reply: Anonymous, "Does a Passion for Growing Food Mean a Life of Poverty? Response to a NYTimes Op-ed," Southern Maryland Agricultural Development Commission, September 11, 2014, https://smadc.com/does -a-passion-for-growing-food-mean-a-life-of-poverty-response-to-a -nytimes-op-ed/.

36. I talked to Eric Glasgow by phone December 9, 2016.

37. Michael Idov, "Bitter Brew. I Opened a Charming Neighborhood Coffee Shop. Then It Destroyed My Life," Slate, http://www.slate.com/id/2132576.

38. Grant McCracken, *Dark Value: How to Find Hidden Value in the Digital Economy* (New York: Periph.: Fluide, 2016). See thoughts from Sam Ford on the tensions between commodity and gift economies here: Grant McCracken and Sam Ford, "Project Entry #2: The Peacefield Farms Interview," *The Artisanal Economies Project* (blog), April 29, 2017, https://artisanaleconomiesproject.org/2017/04/29/the-artisanal-economies-project-entry-2-the-peacefield-farms-interview/.

39. Taffy Brodesser-Akner, "How Goop's Haters Made Gwyneth Paltrow's Company Worth $250 Million," *New York Times*, July 25, 2018, https://www.nytimes.com/2018/07/25/magazine/big-business-gwyneth-paltrow-wellness.html.

40. I interviewed Mateo on the phone November 20, 2020.

41. Carl Bialik, "Numbersguy Blog: Starbucks Stays Mum on Drink Math," *Wall Street Journal*, April 2, 2008, https://www.wsj.com/articles/BL-NB-309.

42. Barry Schwartz, *The Paradox of Choice: Why More Is Less* (New York: Ecco, 2003).

43. Nicholas Carr, *The Shallows: What the Internet Is Doing to Our Brains* (New York: W. W. Norton, 2011); Mark Bauerlein, *The Dumbest Generation: How the Digital Age Stupefies Young Americans and Jeopardizes Our Future* (New York: Tarcher, 2009).

44. Steve Pinker, *Enlightenment Now: The Case for Reason, Science, Humanism, and Progress* (New York: Penguin, 2019).

45. Max Weber, "Science as Vocation," in *From Max Weber: Essays in Sociology*, edited by H. H. Gerth and C. Wright Mills (New York: Oxford University Press, 1946), pp. 129–56.

46. I am indebted to Pip Coburn for his thoughts, and our conversations, on personalization.

47. Kendi and DiAngelo have thought a lot about this task; Ibram X. Kendi, *How to Be an Antiracist* (New York: One World, 2019); Robin DiAngelo and Michael Eric Dyson, *White Fragility: Why It's So Hard for White People to Talk about Racism*, reprint ed. (Boston: Beacon Press, 2018).

48. Next time the music and culture festival called Afropunk comes to town, go. https://afropunk.com.

49. Anonymous, "Volunteering in America Report Finds Increase in Volunteering and Civically-Related Activities," AmeriCorps, November 13. 2018, https://www.nationalservice.gov/newsroom/press-releases/2018/volunteering-us -hits-record-high-worth-167-billion; Anonymous, "Giving Statistics," Charity Navigator, n.d., https://www.charitynavigator.org/index.cfm?bay=content .view&cpid=42.

50. Grant McCracken, "Screw the Gift Economy, a Reply to Clay Shirky," CultureBy, December 15, 2015, https://cultureby.com/2015/12/screw-the -gift-economy-a-reply-to-clay-shirky-html.

51. Mark Fedeli, "Agricultural Revolution: Farm Hotels Are Growing Up," part 2: "The New World," "Blackberry Farm," Tablet: The Agenda, March 23, 2018, https://magazine.tablethotels.com/en/2018/03/agricultural -revolution/.

52. It looks like the Heritage Tea House has been overwhelmed by current affairs and the coronavirus. Its long-term status is unclear. I am waiting to do a follow-up interview with Raeisha.

53. Heritage has suffered the effects of COVID. It is suspended, perhaps closed down. Details forthcoming.

54. Anonymous, "About Us," The Flowers and Bread Society, n.d., https://www .flowersandbread.com/pages/about-us.

55. Frank Giustra, "Welcome to the Million Gardens Movement," ModernFarmer .com, n.d., https://modernfarmer.com/million-gardens-movement/.

56. Thanks to Scott Gilmore at Modern Farmer for an illuminating interview, December 14, 2020.

57. This passage taken from the Facebook passage of Tyson Gersh: https://www .linkedin.com/in/tysongersh/.

58. Tom Perkins, "On Urban Farming and 'Colonialism' in Detroit's North End Neighborhood," *Detroit Metro Times*, December 20, 2017, https://www .metrotimes.com/detroit/on-urban-farming-and-colonialism-in-detroits -north-end-neighborhood/Content?oid=7950059.

59. Anonymous. "Artisanal Chewing Gum Factory," Thrillist, October 25, 2010, http://www.thrillist.com/bayswater/food-dining/2010/10/22/artisanal -chewing-gum-factory.

60. Levine and Heimerl (eds.), *Handmade Nation*; Levine (director) and Heimerl (producer), *Handmade Nation*.

61. Levine, "Preface," in Levine and Heimerl (eds.), *Handmade Nation*, p. xi.

62. Susan Beal, "Craft Fairs Redux," in Levine and Heimerl (eds.), *Handmade Nation*, pp. 121–25.

63. Kathleen Habbley in Beal, "Craft Fairs Redux," p. 122.

64. Christy Petterson, Sharon Mulkey, and Susan Voelker in Beal, "Craft Fairs Redux," pp. 122–23.

65. Mark Granovetter, "Economic Action and Social Structure: The Problem of Embeddedness," *American Journal of Sociology* 91 (3): 481–510; Karl Polanyi, *The Great Transformation*, foreword by Robert M. MacIver (New York: Farrar & Rinehart, 1944).

66. Charles Coolidge Parlin, *Department Store Lines* (Philadelphia: Curtis, 1912). This idea has been endlessly recycled. Poor A. G. Lafley, twice the CEO of P&G, witlessly made "consumer is boss" his mantra. Anonymous, "A.G. Lafley," n.d., https://en.wikipedia.org/wiki/A.G._Lafley.

67. McNamee, *Alice Waters and Chez Panisse*, Kindle location 827.

68. And this leads to a tension as artisans look for the balance of work that is crowd-pleasing and work that is true to the artisan's art.

69. Tyler Cowen, "Automation Alone Isn't Killing Jobs," *New York Times*, April 6, 2014, accessed September 13, 2014, http://www.nytimes.com/2014/04/06/business/automation-alone-isnt-killing-jobs.html. See also Erik Brynjolfsson and Andrew McAfee, *Race Against The Machine: How the Digital Revolution Is Accelerating Innovation, Driving Productivity, and Irreversibly Transforming Employment and the Economy* (Digital Frontier Press, 2011).

70. Nick Reding, *Methland: The Death and Life of an American Small Town* (New York: Bloomsbury USA, 2009).

71. Ryan Tate, "Blue Bottle Cashes In on Coffee Authenticity," *Wired*, October 2012, accessed October 26, 2014, http://www.wired.com/2012/10/blue-bottle-cashes-in/.

72. For a middle-ground approach: John Peabody, "Moneybox: How to Scale Your Artisanal Business in Four Easy Steps," Slate, October 30, 2014, http://www.slate.com/blogs/moneybox/2014/10/30/how_to_make_an_artisanal_business_scalable.html.

73. I am sorry to say that I am unable to identify the source of this story. I read it years and years ago.

74. Kevin Kelly, a writer and beekeeper in Pacifica, in Frauenfelder, *Made by Hand*, p. 164.

75. Linda Hedman Beyus and Sam Dangremond, "How Two Manolo Blahnik Executives Became Award-Winning Dairy Farmers," *Town & Country*, June 26, 2017, https://www.townandcountrymag.com/leisure/dining/a10041551/arethusa-farm-and-dairy/.

76. David Rees, "Artisanal Pencil Sharpener, YouTube, April 11, 2012, https://youtu.be/spMaP-_Cq_8.

77. Eliza Barclay, "'Bespoke Water' Video Pokes Fun at Earnest Artisanal Food Makers," NPR, August 5, 2015, https://www.npr.org/sections/thesalt/2015/08/05/429031666/bespoke-water-video-pokes-fun-at-earnest-artisanal-food-makers. For an illuminating treatment of a company dedicated to artisanal kindling, see this earnest treatment of the Smoke & Flame firewood company, "North America's only premium handcrafted firewood manufacturer": https://youtu.be/TBb9O-aW4zI.

78. McDonald's McCafé ad, https://youtu.be/KraleWAiKvE.

79. Raphael Brion, "Watch Lewis Black Slam the 'Artisanal' Food Trend," *Eater*, May 2, 2012, https://www.eater.com/2012/5/2/6590799/watch-lewis-black-slam-the-artisanal-food-trend.

80. Fred Armisen and Carrie Brownstein, "Colin the Chicken," *Portlandia*, December 1, 2017, https://www.youtube.com/watch?v=G_PVLB8Nm4.

81. David E. Shi, *The Simple Life: Plain Living and High Thinking in American Culture* (New York: Oxford University Press, 1985).

82. Robert Potts, "An Adaptable Gather: The Revival of the Penguin Modern Poets Series," *Times Literary Supplement*, no. 4814, July 7, 1995, p. 31; Ted Polhemus, *Street Style: From Sidewalk to Catwalk* (London: Thames & Hudson, 1994), p. 9; Jason Fine, "The Hardstuff: Are the Chemical Brothers Techno's First Rock Stars?", Option 72, no. (January 1997): 62; Clifford Geertz, "Blurred Genres: The Refiguration of Social Thought," in *Local Knowledge: Further Essays in Interpretive Anthropology* (New York: Basic Books, 1983), pp. 20, 21.

83. Aristotle in Arlene W. Saxonhouse, *Fear of Diversity: The Birth of Political Science in Ancient Greek Thought* (Chicago: University of Chicago Press, 1992), p. 15.

84. Isaiah Berlin, "Alleged Relativism in Eighteenth-Century European Thought," in *The Crooked Timber of Humanity* (New York: Fontana Press, 1990), p. 90.

85. See the Wikipedia entry for Heraclitus here: https://en.wikipedia.org/wiki/Heraclitus.

86. Reding, *Methland*; Sam Quinones, *Dreamland: The True Tale of America's Opiate Epidemic* (New York: Bloomsbury Press, 2015).

87. Grant McCracken, "Project Entry #10: Bee Keeping with Dr. Christoph Ohngemach," *The Artisanal Economies* Project (blog), June 26, 2017, https://artisanaleconomiesproject.org/2017/06/26/project-entry-10-bee-keeping-with-dr-christoph-ohnegemach/.

88. Colin Dwyer, "Sacklers Withdrew Nearly $11 Billion from Purdue As Opioid Crisis Mounted," NPR, December 17, 2019, https://www.npr.org/2019/12/17/788783876/sacklers-withdrew-nearly-ll-billion-from-purdue-as-opioid-crisis-mounted.

89. David Epstein, *Range: Why Generalists Triumph in a Specialized World* (New York: Riverhead Books, 2019).

90. https://www.warren-wilson.edu/programs/ma-in-craft/.

91. This paragraph has been adapted from Grant McCracken, "The Intrinsic Economy," CultureBy, August 4, 2016, https://cultureby.com/2016/08/the-intrinsic-economy-why-the-republicans-must-lose-in-the-long-term.html.

CHAPTER 6

THE MOMENT: CRAFT IN THE TIME OF COVID

1. Anonymous, "Epson America Introduces 'Artisan'—New Flagship Line of Premium Ink Jet All-in-Ones That Combine Power and Performance with Sleek and Chic Styling," press release, https://news.epson.com/news/Artisan_Release.

2. Dana Steinberg, "Rebuilding the U.S. Economy: One Heirloom Tomato at a Time," Wilson Center, April 2011, https://www.wilsoncenter.org/article/rebuilding-the-us-economy-one-heirloom-tomato-time.

3. In Community Supported Agriculture consumers agree to buy some or all of their produce from a local farmer. More formally, "growers and consumers [provide] mutual support and [share] the risks and benefits of food production." Anonymous, "Community Supported Agriculture," USDA National Agricultural Library, https://www.nal.usda.gov/afsic/community-supported-agriculture#. By 2012, the number of CSAs was sixty-five hundred. By April 2020, it was thirteen thousand. Steven McFadden, "Unraveling the CSA Number Conundrum," Deep Agroecology, 2012, https://deepagroecology.org/2012/01/09/unraveling-the-csa-number

-conundrum/; Hannah Ricker and Mara Karda-Nelson, "Community Supported Agriculture Is Surging amid the Pandemic," April 9, 2020, https://civileats.com/2020/04/09/community-supported-agriculture-is-surging-amid-the-pandemic/.

4. Anonymous, "Year in Food: Artisanal Out As Apps Get Hype," CBS News, December 22, 2010, https://www.cbsnews.com/news/year-in-food-artisanal-out-as-apps-get-hype/.

5. Jen Doll, "Artisanal, Reluctant Branding Pioneer, Dies at Age 474," *The Atlantic,* May 30, 2012, https://www.theatlantic.com/culture/archive/2012/05/artisanal-reluctant-branding-pioneer-dies-at-age-474/327491/.

6. Jen Doll, "Artisanal Won't Die," *The Atlantic*, April 3, 2013, https://www.theatlantic.com/national/archive/2013/04/artisanal-wont-die/316659/.

7. A.C.S., "The Return of Artisanal Employment, The Economist, October 11, 2011, https://www.economist.com/free-exchange/2011/10/31/the-return-of-artisanal-employment#. (P. H. Kapp makes the argument several years later: "The Artisan Economy and Post-industrial Regeneration in the US," *Journal of Urban Design* 22 (4) (2017): 47793, https://doi.org/10.1080/13574809.2016.1167588; Paul Solman, "Could Brooklyn Hipsters Help Save the Middle Class?", *PBS NewsHour,* July 10, 2014, https://www.youtube.com/watch?v=8xHun6klxvA#t=490, Andrew Ward, "Can Hipsters and the Artisan Economy Save the Middle Class?", *Daily Finance,* July 17, 2014, http://www.dailyfinance.com/2014/07/17/can-hipsters-artisan-economy-save-middle-class/. See also Joseph Berger, "N.Y. / Region: Small Factories Thrive in Brooklyn, Replacing Industrial Giants," *New York Times*, August 7, 2012, http://www.nytimes.com/2012/08/08/nyregion/small-factories-thrive-in-brooklyn-replacing-industrial-giants.html.

8. Sabrina Tavernise and Sarah Mervosh, "U.S.: America's Biggest Cities Were Already Losing Their Allure. What Happens Next?", *New York Times*, April 19, 2020, https://www.nytimes.com/2020/04/19/us/coronavirus-moving-city-future.html.

9. Alissa Morris in Sara Morrow, "The (Not So) Simple Life," *Modern Farmer* 10 (Winter 2015): 74.

10. Staff, Pacific Standard, "Americans' Diets Are (a Little Bit) Better Than They Were 15 Years Ago," *Pacific Standard*, June 21, 2016, accessed September 30, 2020, https://psmag.com/news/americans-diets-are-a-little-better-than-they-were-15-years-ago.

11. Anonymous, "2019 Organic Survey Results Show Sales Up 31% from 2016," news release, United States Department of Agriculture, October 22, 2020, https://www.nass.usda.gov/Newsroom/2020/10-22-2020.php, number rounded.

12. Craig Smith, "70 Amazing Etsy Statistics," DMR, March 15, 2015, with updates, https://expandedreamblings.com/index.php/etsy-statistics/. I am grateful to Steve King of EmergentResearch.com for sharing his thoughts on the artisanal economy.

13. Amber Burton, "Markets: Etsy and Shopify Buoyed As Covid-19 Boosts Online Sales," *Wall Street Journal*, December 23, 2020, https://www.wsj.com/articles/etsy-and-shopify-buoyed-as-covid-19-boosts-online-sales-11608719401, numbers rounded.

14. *Waiting for Guffman*, directed by Christopher Guest, written by Christopher Guest and Eugene Levy, produced by Castle Rock Entertainment et al. To hear Corky's speech in full: *Waiting for Guffman*-Corky's Speech, YouTube, https://www.youtube.com/watch?v=De6AkndwRpM.

15. Kevin Zimmerman, "Goodbye City Life: Litchfield County Booming Due to NY Exodus," *Westfair Communications* (blog), August 3, 2020, https://westfaironline.com/126353/goodbye-city-life-litchfield-county-booming-due-to-ny-exodus/; Mihir Zaveri, "A Violent August in N.Y.C.: Shootings Double, and Murder Is Up by 50%," *New York Times*, September 2, 2020, https://www.nytimes.com/2020/09/02/nyregion/nyc-shootings-murder.html; Emma G. Fitzsimmons and Dana Rubinstein, "150 Big Businesses Warn Mayor of 'Widespread Anxiety' over N.Y.C.'s Future," *New York Times*, September 10, 2020, https://www.nytimes.com/2020/09/10/nyregion/de-blasio-economy-coronavirus.html.

16. Dana Rubinstein, "New York: De Blasio Vows for First Time to Cut Funding for the N.Y.P.D.," *New York Times*, June 7, 2020, https://www.nytimes.com/2020/06/07/nyregion/deblasio-nypd-funding.html.

17. James Altuchur, "NYC Is Dead Forever," *New York Post*, August 17, 2020, https://nypost.com/2020/08/17/nyc-is-dead-forever-heres-why-james-altucher/.

18. Azi Paybarah, Matthew Bloch, and Scott Reinhard, "New York: Where New Yorkers Moved to Escape Coronavirus," *New York Times*, May 17, 2020, https://www.nytimes.com/interactive/2020/05/16/nyregion/nyc-coronavirus-moving-leaving. html.

19. Zimmerman, "Goodbye City Life."

20. Ellen Barry, "U.S.: The Virus Sent Droves to a Small Town. Suddenly, It's Not So Small," *New York Times*, September 26, 2020, https://www.nytimes.com/2020/09/26/us/coronavirus-vermont-transplants.html.

21. Sara B. Franklin, "Real Estate: Kingston: A City Remade by the Coronavirus," *New York Times*, August 14, 2020, https://www.nytimes.com/2020/08/14/realestate/kingston-coronavirus-new-residents.html.

22. In this research fifty qualitative interviews and five hundred quantitative ones were conducted in late June and July of 2020. The research was covered in several places, especially in Jillian Kramer, "How Covid-19 Is Changing the Way Mothers Parent Their Daughters," *Washington Post*, November 2, 2020, https://www.washingtonpost.com/lifestyle/2020/10/30/mothers-raise-kind-daughters-covid/, and Clare Ansberry, "How Covid-19 Lockdowns Have Boosted Mother-Daughter Bonds—WSJ," *Wall Street Journal*, September 22, 2020, https://www.wsj.com/articles/how-covid-19-lockdowns-have-boosted-mother-daughter-bonds-11600804296.

23. Barry, "The Virus Sent Droves to a Small Town."

24. Contact me for the full report: grant27@gmail.com.

25. Jed Kolko in Tavernise and Mervosh, "America's Biggest Cities Were Already Losing Their Allure."

26. Lisa Kay Solomon, "Making Futures Tangible," Medium, May 12, 2019, https://medium.com/@lisakaysolomon/making-futures-tangible-b2aceabe2017.

27. Andrew Van Dam, "The Unluckiest Generation in U.S. History," *Washington Post*, June 5, 2020, https://www.washingtonpost.com/business/2020/05/27/millennial-recession-covid/.

28. Janet Adamy, "US: Millennials Slammed by Second Financial Crisis Fall Even Further Behind," *Wall Street Journal*, August 9, 2020, https://www.wsj.com/articles/millennials-covid-financial-crisis-fall-behind-jobless-11596811470.

29. Tavernise and Mervosh, "America's Biggest Cities Were Already Losing Their Allure."

30. Jack Kelly, "New Yorkers Are Leaving the City in Droves: Here's Why They're Moving and Where They're Going," *Forbes*. September 5, 2019, https://www.forbes.com/sites/jackkelly/2019/09/05/new-yorkers-are-leaving-the-city-in-droves-heres-why-theyre-moving-and-where-theyre-going.

31. Sabrina Tavernise and Sarah Mervosh, "America's Biggest Cities Were Already Losing Their Allure. What Happens Next?", *New York Times*, April 19, 2020,

sec. U.S. https://www.nytimes.com/2020/04/19/us/coronavirus-moving
-city-future.html.

32. The Merriam-Webster definition of "humblebrag": https://www.merriam
-webster.com/dictionary/humblebrag.

33. Fiona Duncan, "Normcore: Fashion for Those Who Realize They're One
in 7 Billion," *The Cut*, February 2014, http://nymag.com/thecut/2014/02
/normcore-fashion-trend.html.

34. "Sunday Candy," Surf, artist: Donnie Trumpet & The Social Experiment,
featuring Jamila Woods, produced by The Social Experiment, written by
Patrick Paige II, Franco Davis, Jack Red, Macie Stewart, Nico Segal, Chance
the Rapper, Nate Fox, Eryn Allen Kane, Peter CottonTale, J. P. Floyd, Sima
Cunningham, Stix, and Jamila Woods, full lyrics at https://genius.com
/Donnie-trumpet-and-the-social-experiment-sunday-candy-lyrics.

35. "Familiar," Surf, Donnie Trumpet & The Social Experiment, featuring King
Louie & Quavo, produced by The Social Experiment, written by Dustin
Green, Jack Red, Nico Segal, Chance the Rapper, Nate Fox, Peter CottonTale,
J. P. Floyd, Sir The Baptist, Ilan Kidron, King Louie, and Quavo, full lyrics at
https://genius.com/Donnie-trumpet-and-the-social-experiment-familiar
-lyrics.

36. "Wanna Be Cool," Surf, Donnie Trumpet & The Social Experiment, Featuring
Jeremih, KYLE & Big Sean, produced by The Social Experiment, written by
Jeff "Gitty" Gitelman, Cam O'bi, Jack Red, KYLE, Nico Segal, Kiara Lainer,
Chance the Rapper, Nate Fox, Jeremih, Big Sean, Eryn Allen Kane, Peter
Cotton Tale, and Carter Lang.

37. The Jack Reacher novels are written by Lee Child. See Abell's tweet here:
https://twitter.com/StigAbell/status/947231929610461184.

38. See Stig Abell's podcast here: https://podcast.apple.com/gb/podcast/stig
-abells-guide-to-reading/id1535641697. See Season 1, episode 3, for thoughts
on what a book should have to engage, especially circa 7:36. See Season 1,
episode 7, for his thoughts on historical fiction. See Season 1, episode 4, for
the useful similarities between Abell's forthright style and that of his guest
James O'Brien.

39. Joseph A. Schumpeter, *Can Capitalism Survive?: Creative Destruction and the
Future of the Global Economy* (New York: Harper Perennial Modern Classics,
2009); Alvin Toffler, *Future Shock* (New York: Bantam, 1984); Peter Schwartz,
The Art of the Long View: Planning for the Future in an Uncertain World (New York:

Currency Doubleday, 1996); Clayton M. Christensen, *The Innovator's Dilemma: When New Technologies Cause Great Firms to Fail* (Boston: Harvard Business School Press, 1997); Nassim Nicholas Taleb, *The Black Swan: The Impact of the Highly Improbable*, 2nd ed. (New York: Random House Trade, 2010).

40. Christian Lorentzen, "Why the Hipster Must Die," *Time Out*, May 30, 2007, http://newyork.timeout.com/things-to-do-this-week-in-new-york/8355/why-the-hipster-must-die.

41. See the Bud Light TV commercial here: https://www.ispot.tv/ad/dDwM/bud-light-bud-lights-for-everyone.

42. The world-renouncing impulse encourages people to retreat from the world, sometimes to enter religious orders. It was considered by the German sociologist Max Weber. Robert N. Bellah, "Max Weber and World-Denying Love: A Look at the Historical Sociology of Religion," *Journal of the American Academy of Religion* 67, no. 2 (June 1999): 277–304.

43. Erving Goffman, *The Presentation of Self in Everyday Life* (Harmondsworth: Penguin, 1959).

44. For more on multiple selves: Grant McCracken, *Transformations: Identity Construction in Contemporary Culture* (Bloomington: Indiana University Press, 2008). Some people would prefer to talk about different aspects of the self. "Different selves" feels just a little overreaching. But I think it especially applies when we find ourselves hosts to quite and perhaps entirely different points of view.

45. Fernand Braudel, *Civilization and Capitalism, 15th–18th Century*, vol. I: *The Structure of Everyday Life* (Berkeley, CA: University of California Press), p. 323.

CHAPTER 7

THE FUTURE: A NEW ARTISANAL ECONOMY

1. Take the case of the engineers at Carbon Engineering who claim to perform carbon capture at around $100 a ton. Anonymous, "Bill Gates–Backed Carbon Capture Plant Does the Work of 40 Million Trees," CNBC, https://www.youtube.com/watch?v=XHX9pmQ6m_s; anonymous, "Carbon Engineering Pioneering Direct Air Capture of CO2," Carbon Engineering, https://carbonengineering.com/.

2. This is a little like the profile of Apple computers. They only make up 10 percent of the computers in the United States, but they attract most of the attention.

NOTES

3. Grant McCracken, *The New Honor Code* (New York: Simon & Schuster, 2020).

4. Miles Raymer, "Meet 11 Indie Sneaker Labels Changing the Game," Nylon, n.d., https://www.nylon.com/best-indie-sneakers.

5. See Annie Mohaupt's work at https://www.mohop.com and on Season 1, episode 1, of *Handcrafted America*, the TV show hosted by Jill Wagner, https://www.insp.com/shows/handcrafted-america/.

6. Thanks to Laurent Rejto of the Hudson Valley Film Commission for his prompt and generous kindness. For more details, see the website here: www.hudsonvalleyfilmcommission.org.

7. Sinead Bovell, "I Am a Model and I Know That Artificial Intelligence Will Eventually Take My Job," *Vogue*, accessed January 13, 2021, https://www.vogue.com/article/sinead-bovell-model-artificial-intelligence.

8. More on my approach: www.mapping-the-future.com.

9. The play *Mousetrap* opened in London in 1952 and closed in 2020, staging over twenty-eight thousand performances, https://en.wikipedia.org/wiki/The_Mousetrap. Mysie Monte played her part for twelve and a half years. When asked why she left the play, Ms. Monte said, "I think I have earned a rest." https://en.wikipedia.org/wiki/Mysie_Monte.

INDEX

Page numbers in *italics* refer to photographs and illustrations.

INDEX

INDEX